THE GLASTONBURY ZODIAC
& EARTH MYSTERIES UFOLOGY

The Making of a Modern Myth

PAU

AVALONIAN ÆON
PUBLICATIONS

"The Glastonbury Zodiac & Earth Mysteries UFOlogy -
The Making of a Modern Myth"

First Edition published 2015 by
Avalonian Aeon Publications, Glastonbury, England.

ISBN: 978-0-9557696-5-8

A CIP catalogue record for this book is
available from the British Library.

Design and text styling by Bernard Chandler, Glastonbury.
www.graffik.co.uk
Cover image by Yuri Leitch from author's commission.
Based on Aleister Crowley/Lady Frieda Harris Sun tarot card.

Text set in Monotype Plantin 10/12pt
Printed and Bound in Great Britain by
CPI Group (UK) Ltd, Croydon CR0 4YY

DEDICATION

To
Anthony Roberts,
Andrew Collins,
Robert Coon.

ABOUT THE AUTHOR

Paul Weston is the author of *Mysterium Artorius*, *Aleister Crowley and the Aeon of Horus*, and *Avalonian Aeon*. He also published and contributed to the anthology *Signs and Secrets of the Glastonbury Zodiac*. Having majored in Comparative Religion for a Combined Arts degree (which involved a dissertation on Nazi occultism later incorporated into one of his books), Paul went on to work for the Scientology-influenced Institute of Hypnosis and Parapsychology. He eventually became completely absorbed into the Glastonbury matrix and was fortunate to be closely involved in the Psychic Questing work of Andrew Collins. A frequent lecturer, his other main influences and inspirations include Colin Wilson, Dion Fortune, Reiki, Mother Meera, the Fellowship of Isis, Adi Da, John Cowper Powys, Osho, Psychogeography, Gurdjieff, Anthony Robbins, and UFOlogy. He affirms the 2012 gnosis.

www.paulwestonglastonbury.com
www.avalonianaeon.com
www.aleistercrowley666.co.uk
www.mysteriumartorius.co.uk
www.avalonianaeon.blogspot.com
http://www.blogtalkradio.com/paul-weston1
www.facebook.com/AvalonianAeonPublications

ACKNOWLEDGEMENTS

Andrew Collins. For guiding me through a life-changing vision quest that demonstrated for me that the Glastonbury Temple of the Stars is packing some voltage regardless of the consensus truth that it doesn't exist. For allowing me to be the first person to give an extended account of his own amazing adventures there and how they led to the Giza plateau.
www.andrewcollins.com

Jan Roberts. For inviting me to write an introduction to a new edition of *Glastonbury: Ancient Avalon, New Jerusalem* and allowing me to read *Giants in the Earth*, the two major stimuli for this work, and for answering many questions and supplying recollections of luminous events missing from other narratives.

Robert Coon. For huge inspiration and a number of remarkable synchronistic events during the nineties.
www.earthchakras.org

Yuri Leitch. For his usual superb rendition of my image for a book cover.
www.yurileitch.co.uk

Leila Castle. For appearing on the cosmic radar at exactly the right time and providing all the necessary signs.

I must also give credit to *David Clarke* and *Andy Roberts'* outstanding book *Flying Saucerers* for a wealth of detail on British fifties and sixties UFOlogy.

CONTENTS

PREFACE 1

OLD STRAIGHT TRACKS 5

THE MALTWOOD MYSTERIUM 6

REALITY CHECK 10

ATLANTIS OF THE HEART 13

THE GREAT LESLIE AND ADAMSKI DOUBLE-ACT 14

FANTASTIC REALISM 18

SKY PEOPLE 20

LEYS AND UFOs 22

A RADIANT IMMORTAL IN THE SUMMER OF LOVE 24

THE FLYING SAUCER VISION 27

SHAPESHIFTING: MAGONIA AND MARY 32

THE VIEW OVER 1969 37

THE STARMAN AND A FREE FESTIVAL 42

ANTHONY ROBERTS: SOWER OF THUNDER 44

THE OMEGA POINT & THE EMBRYOGENESIS OF THE WORLD SENSORIUM 48

INVOCATION 52

ANCIENT AVALON, NEW JERUSALEM 53

EGYPT AND IMMORTALITY 55

DARK GODS 56

LORD OF THE FLAME 60

ELLIPTICAL NAVIGATIONS 61

LEY LINES AND LANDSCAPE ZODIACS IN QUESTION 65

AEGYPT: THE STAR TEMPLE AND THE GIZA PLATEAU 68

CONVERGENCE 87

GLIMPSES OF ETERNITY 89

VISION QUEST 90

ADDENDUM: THE CONTACT CONUNDRUM 92

AFTERWORD 102

APPENDIX: ANUBIS AT BURROW MUMP,
ISIS OF AVALON & COSMIC TRIGGER 103

BIBLIOGRAPHY 109

'Every thing possible to be believ'd is an image of truth.'

William Blake. *The Marriage of Heaven and Hell.*

'An acceptance level is the level at which concepts, views and data can be allowed to flow into your mind without being rejected at the outset as being impossible. It does not necessarily mean you accept the ideas or concepts, coming to you as total truth, but that you are prepared to give them house room in your mind. That is what I hope you will do with the perhaps novel and strange ideas advanced in this book. I do not ask you to believe in them. I do ask you not to reject them outright but to let them have the hospitality of your mind for a while.'

Brinsley le Poer Trench. *The Sky People.*

'If ever the heritage of a lost Golden Age could be personified it would be found in the star giants that are strewn across the mysterious Somerset landscape.'

Anthony Roberts. *Sowers of Thunder.*

'The Sun Machine is coming down and we're gonna have a party.'

David Bowie. *Memory of a Free Festival.*

I

PREFACE

The Glastonbury Zodiac and Earth Mysteries UFOlogy is a unique work which gives the first account in print of the life-changing UFO experience of author Anthony Roberts and his wife Janet in 1969. It led to him writing a 300 page manuscript. Provisionally entitled *Giants in the Earth*, it was an incredible blend of ancient astronaut theory, lost continents, and the Glastonbury Zodiac. A large section eventually surfaced as *Atlantean Traditions in Ancient Britain* but the majority of the text remains unpublished.

I became the first person outside the Roberts household to read *Giants* in over 40 years whilst I was working in 2013 on a lengthy introduction to a projected new edition of the seventies anthology *Glastonbury: Ancient Avalon, New Jerusalem* that was edited by Anthony Roberts. I also commissioned artist Yuri Leitch to produce a cover from an idea of mine, a Glastonbury version of the Crowley Sun tarot card that recalled the original anthology. I was extremely pleased with the result.

I realised that *Glastonbury: Ancient Avalon, New Jerusalem*, although not in itself a work of what could be termed Earth Mysteries UFOlogy, arose out of that wider cultural context, the sixties zeitgeist. Its editor believed that the alleged landscape star temple was twelve thousand years old and created by Atlanteans with probable help from aliens. Although that belief is not expressed in the anthology, the knowledge that it was present and helped provide the dynamism that created the work is, I feel, important and interesting.

I began to realise that the two interlinked topics of Atlantis and the UFO mystery, with a consistent sense that there was nothing unidentified involved but was the sign of the presence of intervention in the life of this planet by physical beings from other worlds, were important foundations of the modern Glastonbury mythos and the extent of their influence on the development of the place as modern spiritual capital of Britain and global pilgrimage site is far greater than many might appreciate. These ideas were able to assimilate the existing history and mythology, stories of Arthur, Joseph of Arimathea and the Grail. In a wider context they stimulated a general interest in ancient sites such as Stonehenge and Avebury. If nothing else, a prodigious feat of imagination was involved.

The publication of the new edition of the anthology stalled however but I continued to have faith in the piece and the image that accompanied it. Towards the end of 2014 I was inspired to contact the organisers of the Glastonbury Symposium (still often known as the Crop Circle Conference) with a proposal to give a presentation on the contents of the Introduction. What I hadn't appreciated was that, given that the 2015 event would be the 25th anniversary of the conference, such a retrospective was most welcome.

As the event approached and it seemed unlikely that the anthology would surface in time, I approached a number of significant personal anniversaries. It was also 25 years in June since I experienced a life-changing 36 hour intensive vision quest around the Temple of the Stars led by noted mysteries researcher Andrew Collins. It was 5 years in June since my extensive account of these adventures had been published in my *Avalonian Aeon*. I started to feel very strongly that the subject was alive and calling out to me again and I needed to acknowledge it. I then realised that my presentation would be 10 years to the day since Andrew Collins had spoken at the same conference on *Gods, Grails, and Morphian Contact*, a rare personal account of his Glastonbury experiences.

I decided to expand my introductory piece, with its treatment of *Giants in the Earth*, Desmond Leslie, Brinsley le Poer Trench, Tony Wedd, and the UFO demonic paranoia of Eric Ingelsby, into a larger book with wider scope that could be well-served by the inclusion of subjects I had tackled before but within a new distinct context.

I looked again with the fresh understanding I had gained from the Roberts UFO experience at what I already knew about the Glastonbury Zodiac and particularly the remarkable adventures of Andrew Collins. Putting everything together revealed a perspective that I felt was exhilarating and worth sharing. What I found most satisfying about my arrangement of material was the establishment of a chronology that placed the development of the works of various visionaries within a timescale perspective. To give a sense of just how expansive what could be termed the star temple gnosis can be I've also included some powerful visualisations used by Andrew Collins and myself that are dense with imagery.

All of my books are in many ways part of one big book. They cross-reference and enhance each other and do feature some common material. *Mysterium Artorius* and *Aleister Crowley and the Aeon of Horus* started life as part of *Avalonian Aeon*. The larger book still contains sections found in its children but within a different context. This work is rooted in *Avalonian Aeon* as well. Its centre of gravity is also the Glastonbury Zodiac and it shares sections on Andrew Collins, Maltwood, Caine, Reiser, Coon, and Tony Roberts, although my reading of *Giants in the Earth* has significantly expanded my perspective on him here.

The section on Robert Coon and Oliver Reiser in the anthology *Sign and Secrets of the Glastonbury Zodiac*, which in turn mostly originated in *Avalonian Aeon*, is included here but has been split up to further the wider chronological narrative. *Aegypt* was also featured in *Signs and Secrets* and is reproduced here in almost identical form. It derives from a far more extensive treatment in *Avalonian Aeon*. UFOlogical material from *Aleister Crowley and the Aeon of Horus* is brought in to expand understanding on the fundamental themes of Contact and fairy lore.

Do I believe in these incredible ideas? I totally understand all the many criticisms that can be brought against them. I clearly state a number of them here. The Glastonbury Zodiac is not there by any standards of archaeology and research. I have had one of the truly great formative experiences of my life traversing it though. Andrew Collins was ultimately led to a spectacular discovery on the Giza plateau from a virtual sci-fi immersion in the landscape. Enter, if you will, for a short while, into the fantastic realism, the soul poetry that the landscape of Glastonbury has inspired and hopefully you may come to appreciate why I am willing to believe that a profoundly mysterious elusive something is at work in the landscape and impacts the psyche through the mutating form of a stellar gnosis.

Paul Weston
Glastonbury.
July 23rd, 'Cosmic Trigger Day' 2015.

5

OLD STRAIGHT TRACKS

'We'll open up the Old Straight Track and fertilise the Earth,
rediscover the healing sound and ride the psychic surf —
We're talking of the labours and the work that must be done,
to purify, to sanctify, to stand inside the sun,
to enter in the Pyramid, to conquer all our fears,
to light the blazing lamp of Love
and shine it bright and clear.'

Steve Hillage. *Electric Gypsies.*

THE MOOD OF SIXTIES AND SEVENTIES Glastonbury was significantly inspired by a number of visionaries working back in the twenties and thirties. Alfred Watkins and Katharine Maltwood, two considerably different people, were the earliest and most obviously influential.

Watkins was a Herefordshire merchant who travelled the country as part of his work. He developed antiquarian interests and was always fascinated to hear local landscape legends told by members of families who had lived in the same, virtually unchanging locations, for countless generations. This helped prepare his sensibilities for a moment of revelation. In 1921, at Blackwardine, Herefordshire, he was admiring the view when a strange intuition came over him. It was a way of perceiving the landscape differently and it seemed to represent a glimpse of an archaic forgotten worldview. He sensed a web of lines linking holy places and ancient sites: mounds, old stones, crosses, ancient crossroads, churches on pre-Christian sites, legendary trees and holy wells. They all seemed to stand in straight alignments that ran over beacon hills to cairns and mountain tops. When he came to investigate his vision on maps it appeared to be confirmed. Such features fell on straight lines with a frequency he felt to be above chance. Particular names seemed to regularly appear along such alignments: Red, White, Black, Cold, Cole, Dod, Merry and Ley. The last gave the phenomenon the name that's stuck and since travelled the world. *Ley lines.*

Watkins' discoveries were published in the 1925 work, *The Old Straight Track.* It attracted a small group of enthusiasts who formed a Straight Track Postal Portfolio Club and went on picnic-type outings to further his studies. It was all seen as a kind of charmingly eccentric manifestation of the inter-war years. The archaeological establishment barely deemed it necessary to refute the book. Watkins was not alone in looking at prehistoric sites in an unconventional way. At that time the idea of astronomical alignments at places like Stonehenge was already being discussed. It was Watkins who managed to stimulate a wider interest though, and he will always be remembered as the pioneer.

THE MALTWOOD MYSTERIUM

'Knowest though not Asclepius that our land is the image of heaven, the representation on Earth of every celestial ordinance? Our land is the temple of the world.'

Corpus Hermeticum. *Asclepius.*

DURING THE PSYCHEDELIC SIXTIES, when interest in ancient mysteries was being stimulated by the consciousness-shift zeitgeist, Glastonbury inevitably attracted attention. One idea that had been formulated decades before now found that the time was ripe for wider acceptance. This landscape temple of the stars is now generally known as the Glastonbury Zodiac.

If it could only be fully appreciated from the air did that mean it was deliberately constructed not just to make a microcosmic mirror of the heavens on earth but to display to sky deities who might turn out to be extra-terrestrials? A number of years before Erich von Daniken achieved fame, wealth, and notoriety, for his propagation of the theme, ancient astronauts were being invoked in connection with Glastonbury.

All of this inspiration derived from the work of a remarkable woman. Katharine Maltwood indubitably possessed considerable artistic and mystical sensibilities. A sculptress graduate of the Slade School of Fine Art, she was temperamentally inclined to notice potential shapes in broad masses of material and bringing out their details. During the decades either side of the First World War her works were regularly exhibited at the London Salon, Royal Academy, and other London galleries.

Maltwood absorbed Theosophical ideas through her friendship with John M. Watkins, founder of the notable London bookshop, who had known Madame Blavatsky during the last phase of her life when she had lived in London. The meeting was a fond memory to

Watkins of which he would often speak and his shop became a major source of eastern and Theosophical literature. Katharine Maltwood was never an active member of the Theosophical Society, but subscribed to their journals and had articles published therein.

A short passage in Blavatsky's monumental and profoundly difficult work *The Secret Doctrine* was later quoted by Maltwood in her *Enchantments of Britain.* Whether she had noticed it before formulating the theories for which she is best known, or saw it again later and reached a retrospective perspective, it provides a meta-context for her great work. Blavatsky believed that in immemorial antiquity initiates of a primordial wisdom tradition focused in Central Asia had gone walkabout with some kind of zodiac package. A centre was established by one of these groups in the Gobi Desert.

> *'As above so below. Sidereal phenomena, and the behaviour of the celestial bodies in the heavens were taken as a model, and the plan was carried out below on earth. In the same manner and on the plan of the Zodiac in the upper Ocean or the heavens, a certain realm on Earth, an inland sea was consecrated and called "the Abyss of Learning"; twelve centres on it in the shape of twelve small islands representing the zodiacal signs - two of which remained for ages the "mystery signs" and were the abodes of twelve Hierophants and masters of wisdom. This "Sea of Knowledge" or learning remained for ages there.'*

Having married a childhood friend who was a wealthy business-man, Katharine was able to travel widely. A Nile cruise in 1919 saw her photographed sitting on the knees of a statue of Rameses II at Luxor. Her interest in Egypt became an abiding one. She later produced an alabaster group named *Infinity,* also entitled *Isis, Horus and Osiris.* There can be no doubt that the discovery of the tomb of Tutankhamen and the gradual revealing of its treasures would have significantly impacted upon her, leaving an abiding feeling of Egyptian art and culture present in her mind.

After the First World War, the Maltwoods bought a home at Chilton Priory, near the village of Chilton Polden in Somerset, within sight of Glastonbury Tor. It served as a base for their global travels, gradually becoming increasingly significant.

The landscape surrounding Glastonbury attracted Maltwood's attention in connection with a medieval Grail Romance, *The High History of the Holy Grail* or *Perlesvaus*, a text claiming to have drawn on documents in Glastonbury Abbey. Pondering on various mythic beasts featured in the tale, in conjunction with the sense that it featured definite details of local topography, she came to believe in the existence of a series of effigies, generally depicting signs of the zodiac in set sequence with a circumference of about thirty miles.

The configuration included the usual ram, fishes, and a scorpion. The apparent symmetry of the design seems impressive. Firstly, we have zodiacal images in correct sequence pivoting around a central point. The heads of all but one image face west. Winter signs are placed in the north, four of which are partly drawn by the River Brue, summer signs lie in the south, four drawn with the aid of the River Cary. Eight of the effigies are similar in size, approximately 6,000 yards in breadth. There are three human figures in the group, Sagittarius, Virgo, and Gemini, which are taken to represent a father, mother, and child trinity and form an equilateral triangle. If laying a planisphere of the same scale as the landscape zodiacal circle down upon a map, the stars of the various constellations do tend to lie within the bounds of the alleged effigies. This enables one to say that a particular star has a definite corresponding location on the ground. This is the Hermetic "As above, so below" par excellence. Maltwood considered that the design has come together through some extraordinary process in nature that has been recognised and then enhanced through human agency.

This was the true Round Table of Arthur. The king himself was part of it, as the mounted archer of Sagittarius. Here was his original titanic form, asleep in Avalon. It was the Arthur figure that helped Maltwood to determine, at least to her own satisfaction, when the mighty work was constructed and by whom. Sagittarius has been variously linked with ancient deities whose names seem similar to Arthur: ie Assyrian Assur, Persian Ahura, and Phoenician Melkarth. Glastonbury's Sagittarian archer seems to have a bearded face and pointed cap suggesting a middle-eastern look. He is aiming directly at the star Aldebaran, in Taurus. The Mesopotamian rivers Tigris and Euphrates rise at the spring equinox. Today the sun enters Aries at that time. When, due to precession of the equinoxes, it had been in Taurus, Aldebaran was synchronised with the rivers as Sirius once was with the Nile inundation. It began the Babylonian New Year festivities. Katharine Maltwood came to believe that it was during this period, around 2,700BC, that the landscape zodiac was constructed by wandering initiates of some Middle Eastern mystery cult.

There a few differences in the effigy imagery to our modern depictions of the zodiac. The constellation of Cancer effectively lay outside the circle and is not present. The nearby Argo Navis, usually seen as a ship, is part of the group. It would come to be an important factor in subsequent ideas and experiences concerning the star temple.

The biggest difference between the Glastonbury design and conventional zodiacs served as further evidence to Maltwood of its Babylonian provenance. The Aquarian effigy is supposedly in the shape of a phoenix. This figure looms all the more prominently due to its linking with Glastonbury's most notable landmark, the Tor, which forms most of its head. The bird holds the Chalice Well in its beak and this represents the usual Aquarian water pot. Maltwood mentions the tale of the Chaldean bird Zu who forced entry into the chamber of destiny and seized the tablets of fate. Zu was taken to represent Aquarius.

Perhaps the most convincing of all the effigies is not actually part of the zodiacal twelve. There is supposedly a guardian dog of the sacred round table. Its nose is at Burrow Mump, a kind if mini-Tor that some have speculated may be artificial, also with a ruined Michael church on its summit. The nearest town of any size is Langport. An old Somerset song tells how

> *'The Girt Dog of Langport has burnt his long tail*
> *And this is the night we go singing Wassail'.*

"Girt" means large. An impressive number of evocative place names cluster around the area where Maltwood saw the effigy. His tail is at Wagg! There are two Head Droves near his head, Earlake Moor by his ear, *Cur*ry Rivel on a front paw. Even if a huge effigy doesn't exist, these are strong indications of some kind of dog tradition in the vicinity.

In *A Guide to Glastonbury's Temple of the Stars* published in 1935, and *The Enchantments of Britain,* published in 1944 after a move from Britain to Canada, Katharine Maltwood put forward her ideas on the Glastonbury Zodiac and its connection with *Perlesvaus.* A set of aerial photos were also taken for a now rare companion volume. Like Alfred Watkins *Old Straight Track,* academics scarcely registered Maltwood's works. British occultists of the time don't seem to have been particularly aware of her either.

* * *

REALITY CHECK

BEFORE PROCEEDING into the furthest-out zones of the Glastonbury Zodiac mythos it is worth pausing to take stock of some of the diverse elements present in the brew and address consensus concerns at the outset. To begin with, we have the Maltwood interpretation of *Perlesvaus.* Much ink has been expended by critics in search of an understanding of this distinctive text but a zodiacal aspect had yet to be expounded by the time of *Temple of the Stars.* If it is really there, it's buried pretty deep.

Maltwood mentions that the *Quest del San Graal* stated enigmatically that, *'The Round Table was constructed, not without great significance, upon the advice of Merlin. By its name it is meant to signify the round world and round canopy of the planets and the elements in the firmament, where are to be seen the stars and many other things.'* It also mentions the table of the Grail feeding four thousand people and 150 bulls. It was *'in a meadow'*. This does seem to clearly indicate that it covers a large area on the land. It might have been more useful for Maltwood's argument if *Perlesvaus* said something similar so clearly but the quote does hint at strange ideas about the Round Table existing somewhere in the background around the beginning of the thirteenth century.

In the Grail romances and historical documents of the period there are three meanings for the term Round Table. One is the most obvious, a table to eat a meal from. It also means a chivalric institution, an order of knighthood. In that context it will tend to mention large numbers of people. Taken as a whole, the Grail Romances use the term Round Table to describe an institution more often than an eating place, although that's not how later times remember it. The third meaning is that of a tournament of some kind, a pageant, a show, an invocation of chivalry, featuring jousting and feasting. These gatherings were often inspired by the Arthurian mythos. The famous Winchester Round Table may well have been constructed as an accompaniment to such an event. This could be sufficient explanation for the seemingly odd romance references.

Scholars of Maltwood's time believed many things about British pre-Roman history that would now be called into question. Many of her apparently wild theories arose out of such a background of ideas. For example, in *Enchantments of Britain,* she quotes L. A. Waddell from his *Origin of Britons and Scots* who claimed that the Welsh originated in Sumeria. *'We discover that the "Cymry" of*

Wales derive their name from "Sumer"'. Various traders and colonisers had come to ancient Albion by about 2700BC. The Celtic Caer Sidi starlore was a mutated form of the Mesopotamian cultural package. This was a variant on widely stated beliefs of the time. The reputable Arthurian scholar John Rhys considered that Somerset meant "Land of Summer". Druidic material of debatable authenticity spoke of the Cymry being led from the east, from a *'Summer Country over the hazy sea'*. If that wasn't discouraging enough it is a tad unfortunate that one of Waddell's most used words is "Aryan". He is in fact so enthusiastic in his advocacy of it that his works are popular today amongst mystics whose sensibilities could be described as somewhere to the right of centre.

So what was happening in Somerset round about the period when wandering Sumerians are supposed to have disembarked circa 2700BC? There was certainly a lot going on in the area by Neolithic times. Trees were being cleared using axes made from stone seemingly imported from distant locations. Wooden trackways crossed the Somerset Levels through the marshland. These constructions constitute what are essentially amongst the oldest roads in the world, having been individually dated to periods between 3806 to about 2500BC. The tracks had a limited lifespan and were primarily for use during the more flooded times of the year. Cattle were driven across them. Canoes docked at the ends of some. The culture that produced them was obviously well organised and with manpower resources. The people were not isolated. They had contact with the world beyond. Somewhere in the middle of that timescale the Sumerian genesis of civilisation with the wheel, writing, decimal counting etc, can be dated. The famous Glastonbury lake villages were some considerable time later, a few hundred years BC only.

The Sumerians were also pioneer seafarers but could they possibly have travelled as far as Britain? There is a total absence of any archaeological proof here. The best that can be said is that the current absence of proof for Sumerian travellers cannot be equated with impossibility. If they did travel to Somerset they would have found a landscape significantly different from today and this has a major bearing on the Zodiac theory. The issue of the Argo Navis vessel represents the best case in point. It's unique in the Glastonbury Zodiac for a number of reasons. Of all the effigies it's the only one that depicts a man-made object, the rest are animals or humans. It contains straight lines, a feature obviously not found in nature. That implies that, assuming the thing is actually there in the first place, it must have been engineered by humans rather than being some mysterious artwork of Gaia. The problem is that the whole area was marshland until the period from 1790 to 1820. The moors were then drained and rhynes built across the flat area. It's those rhynes that define the ship, so it wasn't there in the medieval period and certainly not in Sumerian times.

Noted Glastonbury author Geoffrey Ashe has always maintained a certain scepticism about the Zodiac. First and foremost, he simply can't see the figures in the land even when they're pointed out to him. He has wondered if an experimental control group were shown various aerial photos of the British landscape that included the Temple of the Stars but were not identified as such that anyone would spontaneously pick out the image of a lion or a boat. Katharine Maltwood was a sculptress after all. She was predisposed to seeing potential shapes in things.

I consider the point to be a valid one. How many people, not already familiar with the Zodiac hypothesis, when seeing an image of the Tor, would say it looked like a phoenix? Some might compare it to Mesopotamian or Mexican step pyramids. The vast majority I'm sure, if pressed to liken it to anything, would probably opt for symbolism of the female form. Local RAF pilots refer to the Tor tower as the "nipple". The Pre-Roman cultures of our islands often linked rolling hills and summits with Goddess figures. It is ideas of this kind that have found far wider response in the recent times.

I'm making it clear here that I am well aware of the tenuous nature of the star temple idea. Something about it however, has somehow catalysed the most extraordinary processes in its adherents. Whilst a few, who I do not mention here, can be considered to be deluded, or even downright crazy, the cases I will expound have in my opinion something remarkable and inspirational about them that may lead the mind to fruitfully think, in Ouspensky's terminology, in *other categories*.

Temple of the Stars did find prestigious support amongst the most elitist of the contemporary European occult cognoscenti. In his short essay, *The Land of the Sun*, Rene Guenon suggested that some of the divergences from the usual zodiacal designs were actually a point in favour of the archaic authenticity of the Glastonbury configuration. Libra is represented by a dove, rather than the usual scales. The bird is placed near the centre of the design at the summit of the converging masts of the Argo Navis ship and could be taken to appear as if flying from the Arthur figure's head. The actual stars of Libra do not fall on the effigy but those of Ursa Major do. Guenon noted that, *'the celestial scales were not always zodiacal, but were at first polar, the name having been applied originally to the Great Bear, or to the Great Bear and Little Bear taken together.'* The axial alignment of the Glastonbury Zodiac is polar. The stars of Ursa Major and Draco the sky serpent, home of the former pole star, are found around its centre. Guenon believed in a Hyperborean primordial polar centre literally once situated at the roof of the world that was the source of the ancient wisdom. With axial displacement and cultural drift, things shifted south into Central Asia and west to what is generally known as Atlantis. Probably prompted by the attention of his onetime mentor Guenon, the Italian fascist magus Julius Evola also accepted the Zodiac, stating in *The Mystery of the Grail* that, *'Glastonbury was itself in prehistoric times a centre of the primordial tradition'.*

ATLANTIS OF THE HEART

ALTHOUGH SEEMINGLY SEPARATE from the work of Watkins and Maltwood, a blend was in the making that would coalesce in the decades to come. The theme of Atlantis was of central importance. The notable occultist and prolific writer Dion Fortune was a great advocate of the special qualities of Glastonbury. Her 1934 work *Avalon of the Heart* evokes the poetic mood that the combination of landscape and legend readily stir in its pilgrims. *'Glastonbury is a spiritual volcano wherein the fire that is at the heart of the British race breaks through and flames to heaven.'*

In a chapter entitled *Avalon and Atlantis,* Fortune wondered if *'there is any possibility that Avalon, with its undercurrent of pagan legend, was originally an Atlantean colony? Is it possible that Merlin was an Atlantean – a priest-initiate; and in presiding at the birth of Arthur he was carrying out the Atlantean custom of the kings bred for wisdom? In order to bring the higher consciousness of the evolved Atlantean race into the Celtic tribes of the colonised island, did Merlin, in defiance of the strict laws of the sacred clan, and in pursuit of ends of his own, cross the Atlantean stock on the Celt, and so breed Arthur? And was Morgan le Fay , the half-sister of Arthur, the witch-woman learned in all sciences, with her name derived from the Celtic word for sea, a pure bred Atlantean, the British-born daughter of the sea people?'* Were the

Atlanteans responsible for the megaliths and ancient tracks? Were the slopes of the Tor sculpted to resemble an Atlantean temple prototype?

Other visionaries also mused upon possible connections between Atlantis and Britain during the period between the wars. John Foster Forbes was fortunate in making use of the talents of two redoubtable female psychics, Olive Pixley and Iris Campbell. Forbes and Pixley visited Glastonbury Tor in 1930. With her eyes open, Pixley saw a ceremony she believed to have Atlantean origins. A group ascended the Tor terraces in pre-dawn twilight in a celebratory manner, involving drumming, singing, and chanting, alongside the backdrop of the sound of children and dogs. Their collective energy created a serpent path of more subtle energy so a spiral spread around the hill. Having reached the summit, where a stone circle stood, their efforts assisted *'a vortex descending from the sun, and the resultant energy shot out through 'the alignments' over the land.'* Nature was stimulated efficaciously in the realms of plants and butterflies. The combination of sound and light was the key. A later collaboration with Iris Campbell in 1945 produced similar results. Forbes and Pixley investigated in their own manner a number of other West Country sites for his 1938 book *The Unchronicled Past.* The Tor vision is typical of Pixley's general work, which clearly anticipates later theories on the presence of a labyrinth there. Thirty years later, Forbes would be a definite influence on John Michell.

THE GREAT LESLIE AND ADAMSKI DOUBLE-ACT

IN THE LATER YEARS of his life John Foster Forbes became enthralled by the UFO mystery and was responsible for organising an event that clearly presages developments a decade later. In September 1954 a picnic occurred amongst the megalithic stones at Avebury. The gathering had a purpose: contact with the Space Brothers. Moving to a vantage point further out in the megalithic landscape, yogic adept George King, who had already been told earlier in the year by a strange voice that he was to *'become the voice of Interplanetary Parliament',* tried his best but was informed by his Native American spirit guide that the mindset of the assembled group, which included a *Daily Mirror* reporter and photographer, was a barrier to communication. Here is a clear example of the ancient 'Atlantean' sites of Britain becoming connected with the lights in the sky. By the end of the year, King had founded the British UFO cult, the Aetherius Society, which survives and thrives in the present day; a glorious mash-up of Theosophy and flying saucers. King's 1958 inspiration to charge up holy mountains with cosmic energy prayer power, that could later be released to heal the planet, anticipated New Age practices by decades.

The Avebury picnic was catalysed by a growing interest in Britain in UFOlogy. The previous year had seen the publication of a sensational work that had broken through from the fringe into the world of the mass media. *Flying Saucers Have Landed* by Desmond Leslie and George Adamski was a perfectly timed mix that would help inspire the alternative culture of the sixties and seventies.

Desmond Leslie was related to Winston Churchill. His family was steeped in ancient history, mysticism, and spiritualism. Brought up in a thoroughly haunted castle home, Leslie went on to such varied activities as wartime spitfire pilot and pioneer of experimental electronic music, creating sounds that would later feature in *Dr Who* and the movie *Dr Strangelove*. It was an experience in 1934, when a child in boarding school, that would lead to his greatest passion. His dormitory had been suddenly lit at night by an *'immense green fireball'* that had generated considerable excitement amongst those present. The memory was re-stimulated with the advent of the flying saucer era in 1947. A spiritualist communication from his dead mother in 1951 further pointed him in the direction of the UFO mystery.

Leslie embarked on a mammoth excursion into a huge mix of unusual literature and started writing. *Flying Saucers Have Landed* began with a survey of some of the recent notable cases and then delved into the back catalogue of strange aerial sightings of which there are many records in the west. In this, he was indebted to the work of Charles Fort, the champion of anomalous data.

The majority of the work's greatest inspiration came from the east however, particularly from the late-nineteenth-century literature of Madame Blavatsky's Theosophy. W. Scott-Elliott's *Atlantis and Lemuria* contained ideas that would become a staple feature of ancient astronaut theory right up to the present day and the *Ancient Aliens* TV series. Hindu literature spoke of *vimanas*, which appeared to be flying craft that fought a sci-fi war in the skies of ancient India. There seemed to be accounts of the equivalent of atomic explosions. The vimanas may even have been able to travel beyond our planet.

Leslie felt that there is '*a strong suggestion that there existed previously, not one but several humanities greater, wiser, more moral, and more advanced in certain aspects of natural science than ourselves.*' In fact '*not one but several inter-planetary migrations from Earth have taken place in the past by means of the vimanas — the site of the last departure was not the Atlantean mainland but Gizeh* [sic] *itself*'. This wild claim is followed by the classic '*I am afraid I can give few references that would be of immediate help in confirming this statement.*'

The kind of literature that Leslie had investigated and the mix he created would prove to be the template for much that was to come. Sunken continents. Ancient technology. The Great Pyramid and the mystery of its construction were considered, with the possibility of a lost art of sound engineering having been employed. Its antiquity was extended before the sinking of Atlantis. The South American site of Tiahuanaco was similarly treated.

In the midst of the heady brew, Leslie looked at Celtic mythological tales of flying chariots, weapons wielded by the Irish hero Cuchulain, and the vitrified stone hill forts of Scotland, interpreting them in the light of the Hindu vimanas, stating that '*Cuchulain is the composite character of a Celtic-Atlantean war lord*'.

Although acknowledging the findings of modern science concerning its somewhat inhospitable physical conditions, Leslie affirmed the unutterably strange but compelling Theosophical lore concerning beings of different vibrational level living on Venus. They care for the human race and have intervened in life on Earth.

Annie Besant and C. W. Leadbetter referred to 'Brahmin Tables' in their *Man, Where, Whence and Whither*, telling how 18,618,793 years ago we experienced contact from Venus. '*Then with the mighty roar of swift descent from incalculable heights, surrounded by blazing masses of fire which filled the sky with shooting tongues of flame, the vessel of the Lords of the Flame flashed through the aerial spaces. It halted over the White Island which lay in the Gobi Sea. Green it was, and radiant with the fairest blossoms as Earth offered her fairest and best to welcome her King.*' Sanat Kumara became Lord of the World and established a base in Shambhala. This concept has been present amongst most of the more well-known New Age teachers from that point onwards.

Leslie concluded his section of the book with the vastly archaic Venus contact story so as to nicely lead into a first-person modern account of what could be taken to be a long-term scenario.

George Adamski remains the most famous and notorious contactee, a man still able to polarise opinion. In November 1952 he claimed to have received a telepathic message calling him to a meeting in the desert with the UFOnauts. Adamski went out with a group into the Mojave, later stating that he had seen a big silver cigar-shaped craft fly by. Asking his friends to stand clear, he moved away on his own to observe a smaller vessel come down and land nearby. A tall long-haired male, looking quite human and wearing some kind of ski-suit came out to make contact. Through telepathy Orthon (as the being was known), gave a warning to the world about the dangers of nuclear power reminiscent of the recent hit movie *The Day the Earth Stood Still.* His people were from Venus. Adamski's account of his story takes up the final fifty pages of *Flying Saucers Have Landed.* The photos he claimed to have taken of the Venusian scout-ship were the most immediate selling-point for the book. There is still much teeth-grinding over them in the present day.

Despite a predictable mauling from the scientific establishment that Leslie seemed to actually enjoy, the book served some general obscure need, becoming a huge success. He appeared on British TV in programmes such as the BBC *Panorama* that gained high viewing figures. Leslie's contacts in the British establishment ensured that the peculiar cultural package his book represented was widely disseminated at a level of society such a work would normally be unlikely to reach so quickly. He knew Battle of Britain hero Hugh Dowding who was likewise taken with UFOs and all manner of mystical beliefs. Dowding would in turn meet Adamski on a British tour. The contactee himself was launched on a truly bizarre journey as international ambassador for the peaceful space people that included a meeting with the Dutch Royal family and various scientists and military men. His later tales, involving personal trips in space ships and innumerable encounters with aliens, seemed increasingly unlikely.

In his introduction to Colin Bennett's Adamski study, *Looking For Orthon*, John Michell wrote that '*He was an impressive old rogue, like Madame Blavatsky and in the same tradition. Such people, according to Plato, are the kind whom the gods choose to enlighten us. I am sure that is right, and that changes in our minds are brought about by the gods, in their due seasons and often through highly dubious characters.*' Leslie sent Adamski a wonderful letter expressing some perplexity.

'I don't know what has happened, George, but all the mediums have suddenly disposed of their Indian guides, etc., and have replaced them with space people traveling in Vimanas.'

One of the greatest thinkers of the twentieth century can help us understand such a peculiar state of affairs. In his famous late work, the 1959 *Flying Saucers: a Modern Myth of Things Seen in the Sky,* C. G. Jung expressed his belief that the UFO phenomenon was an example of *'symptoms of psychic changes that always appear at the end of one Platonic month and at the beginning of another. They are, it seems, changes in the constellation of psychic dominants, of the archetypes, or "gods" as they used to be called, which bring about, or accompany, long-lasting transformations of the collective psyche.'* Ideas that were below the psychic horizon were rising again into consciousness during the transition into the dawning of the new Platonic month or astrological epoch, the Age of Aquarius. Jung was prepared to accept that there was an element of physical reality in some cases but was clear that human consciousness was intimately involved in the process. UFOs were harbingers and accompaniers of much else besides. The sixties would become a legendary decade. The space race, popular music, and drug use, combined to extraordinary effect at the furthest edges of popular culture.

FANTASTIC REALISM

1960 SAW THE PUBLICATION in France of a work that has been considered as perhaps the most significant single impetus for the revival of interest in all things strange. *The Dawn of Magic*, also known as *The Morning of the Magicians*, by Louis Pauwels and Jacques Bergier, would be translated into English by 1963. The authors were an intriguing duo, very much products of French artistic mystical culture, who represented a remarkable blend which was reflected in the contents of their work that, if the level of its success and influence is anything to go by, expressed a lot of what was rising from the depths of the collective unconscious accompanying the things seen in the sky.

Pauwels had studied the work of the fabulously erudite mystical scholar René Guénon and been involved with a Gurdjieff group, authoring a hostile book on the Armenian mage. He had known the founder of the Surrealist movement André Breton. Bergier was trained in physics and fascinated by the art and science of alchemy.

He claimed to have met the legendary Fulcanelli, alchemist author of *The Mystery of the Cathedrals.* There was also time spent in a Nazi concentration camp and alleged involvement in espionage.

The duo spent five years bringing together a surrealist alchemical blend from a wide variety of sources, including the work of Charles Fort, shaping it to help propound an approach they called *fantastic realism*. This involved not an escape from reality but an attempt to see it from a higher perspective where many puzzling oddities could be understood and reconciled. To that end they incorporated the new physics, alchemy and other ancient mysteries, and ideas at the furthest edge of psychology in a relentless mix that served the same purpose as Breton's Surrealism, to subvert consensus reality and assert the primacy of something else. Indeed, the illustrations consisted of an intriguing mix of surrealist and alchemical art alongside the Mayan site of Chichen Itza. The manner of the presentation was a vital part of its effect.

One particular section of the book, entitled *The Vanished Civilisations*, contained a number of ideas that would be tremendously influential in the development of ancient astronaut theory. A group of now familiar favourites were gathered together: mysteries of the construction and dimensions of the Great Pyramid, the huge carved statues of Easter Island, the Nazca desert figures of pre-Incan Peru, the Hindu vimanas that had so enthralled Desmond Leslie. There was also the sixteenth-century Piri Reis maps, apparent indicators of knowledge of an ice-free Antarctica centuries before the continent's discovery. Were they copies of earlier maps that had *'been traced from observations on board a flying machine or space vessel of some kind?' 'We do not reject the possibility of visits from the inhabitants of another world, or of atomic civilizations that vanished without leaving a trace … or of remnants of forgotten sciences surviving in various forms of what is known as esoterism'.*

It was a dense cluster of material that would be sufficient to inspire a whole sub-culture whose most notable exponent remains Erich von Daniken. The fact that *Morning of the Magicians* can be torn to shreds concerning the factual accuracy of a large percentage of its content is important but will not detain us here. For now it is sufficient to register that the work created a particular mood and brought together from a variety of sources a total blend that succeeded in the aim of promoting fantastic realism.

* * *

SKY PEOPLE

THE DISTINCTLY BRITISH expression of the edge of the zeitgeist begun by Desmond Leslie was further developed, essentially simultaneously with Jung, Pauwels, and Bergier, with the work of Brinsley le Poer Trench, who became the Earl of Clancarty, Britain's most prestigious (in terms of social standing) UFO enthusiast. He would eventually use his position in the House of Lords to try and initiate top-level investigation of the subject. An articulate early advocate of the ancient astronaut hypothesis, he was also a champion of Katharine Maltwood and the Glastonbury Zodiac, seeing her work in the context of his own unusual interests.

Trench's first book *The Sky People* was published in 1960. It was a remarkable debut containing ideas that could easily be considered a tad eccentric but have nonetheless achieved longevity and can be recognised with variant details in similar modern works. This indicates that some deeper resonance with the themes it portrays may be at work in the modern psyche.

To begin with, Trench believed that the Garden of Eden story described events that occurred on Mars. There are two creation accounts in *Genesis*. They refer to two different strains of humanity. Adam I, Galactic Man, the Elohim line, has a god-like destiny in the stars that was always intended. This race has been known as the Serpent People and they are the source of the many traditions of culture-bringer deities in human form such as Osiris and Quetzalcoatl. Adam II, the Jehovah line, were the occupants of the original Eden. '*Jehovah then is a name adopted quite recently as such things go, to designate the People from Somewhere Else in space who deliberately created, by means of their genetic science, a race of hu-man beings peculiarly adapted to perform certain definite and predetermined functions.*' They were created as a basic workforce, brute and unthinking, toilers in the garden.

Inevitably, some crossbreeding occurred. This is recalled in the famous lines in *Genesis* concerning the sons of god and the daughters of men. The new strain eventually became predominant. Much of the conflicted nature of the human psyche can be traced back to this dual heritage.

Noah's Ark was a spaceship that transported humans to Earth after the melting of the polar ice cap on Mars caused a flood. Something of this story became part of Atlantean heritage and was later used again, its origins having been forgotten, in relation to the

Earthly deluge that consumed that culture.

Trench's strong background in the mystical history propounded by Madame Blavatsky, involving the lost continents of Atlantis and Mu, along with Desmond Leslie's recent revitalisation, infused his work. Atlantis had spaceships, was in contact with other planets, and used power sources that surpassed nuclear energy. Its prime was in a hugely distant antiquity, up to 30,000 years ago. A sequence of catastrophes over a long period gradually brought it down. An epic war lasting thousands of years caused huge earthquakes and continental upheaval that destroyed most of Atlantis. Inspired by notorious theorist Hans Hoerbiger, Trench avowed that the moon was brought into orbit fairly recently, around 9,500BC, with accompanying upheaval of mountains after a tortuously long period also lasting a few thousand years. It was at the end of that process, that included the raising of the famous site of Tiahuanaco by thousands of feet, that the story that most people associate with Atlantis, where the whole place sinks beneath the sea in a few nights, finally occurred. Some of the elite escaped off-planet and periodically returned to help out the survivors.

Men Among Mankind followed in 1962. The work is notable for its treatment of the work of Katharine Maltwood. Trench had corresponded with her husband John shortly after her death. Britain was part of Atlantis that didn't sink. Trench considerably lengthened the timescale suggested by Maltwood for the construction of the Glastonbury Zodiac. In his version there were Atlanteans who had realised that the final catastrophe was coming, *'and built, in conjunction with the Sky People, a gigantic landmark, which could easily be picked out from the sky on the disrupted surface of the unhappy planet'. 'A legacy from their Atlantean forebears which is infinitely greater than either Stonehenge or the Great Pyramid in Egypt', 'the most sacred spot on Earth'.*

Trench interpreted certain features of the Glastonbury configuration to support the *Sky People* cosmology. The fact that only one of the twins of Gemini is represented implies that the other is in the sky and thereby reminds us that *'the original sense of the Somerset Zodiac was, in part at least, to keep in the memories of the Men of two planets a purpose, a promise, and a prophecy. The purpose, to maintain a connection between two parts of a race – that of Man – which had to be separated for a time: The promise that those separated parts would in time come together again to their mutual benefit: And the prophecy of the date and time of that coming back into communication.' 'If, as we are told, the Age of Aquarius is to be the age of the Regeneration of Man, it is to Glastonbury and to the Temple of the Stars that we must look for information regarding our immediate future.'*

From Britain, the world was civilised again. Here was something of the sensibilities suggested by another Atlantean enthusiast, William Blake, when he said that *'All things begin and end in Albion's ancient Druid rocky shore.'* As part of his advocacy of British pre-eminence, Trench suggested that Egyptian adepts, heirs to Atlantis themselves, travelled to Britain to seek out the knowledge of the most important place on the planet.

'Is it not feasible that the knowledge Osiris and his companions brought back from Britain, given them by those who were in a position to impart it at the most respected and sacred place on earth – the Temple of the Stars in Somerset – formed at least part of the groundwork upon which the Great Pyramid came to be built some millennia later?'

Men Among Mankind must rate as the first clear expression of the sixties Glastonbury cosmic millennialism that would ultimately lead to the transformation of the town into the spontaneous mystical social experiment it now represents. It would be republished as *Temple of the Stars* in 1973.

Trench also expressed a belief in *The Sky People* that had been present in variant forms since the early days of UFOlogy in the aftermath of Hiroshima. *'This planet will not be allowed to blow itself up—the world will not end tomorrow! Whatever the prophets of Doom may say, the elder brothers will not permit this to happen. There is every hope that a nuclear war will not occur. Foreseeing humanity's technological advances, large numbers of extra-terrestrials have come back to help at this critical period of Earth's history. They have reincarnated in human bodies. Numerous Cross-Men, too, are now Galactic dominant. Many of them are still 'sleepers', not yet or only partially awakened, but soon they will be aware of their potentialities.'* It was a theme that the coming hippie years would see intensified when a number of people would wonder if they were Galactic Dominant types in the process of reawakening and it has continued on to the mystical apocalypse of 2012 and beyond.

LEYS AND UFOS

DURING THE SAME formative period of time at the start of the sixties, other ideas that were to link ancient British sites with UFOs were being formulated. Following a sustained season of sightings in

France in 1954, Aime Michell came to believe that the lights in the sky seemed to move in a definite pattern. His book *Flying Saucers and the Straight-Line Mystery* led British enthusiast Tony Wedd, who had seen a UFO as far back as 1941, to wonder if they used ley lines to navigate by.

Tony Wedd was born in Somerset in 1919 and became aware of the Glastonbury Zodiac concept as a young man, walking the landscape around Langport where the guardian dog figure supposedly can be found. Whilst serving in the RAF, Wedd was posted to Canada in 1943 and actually met Katharine Maltwood. Only a modest record remains of their conversation but she speculated that Wedd was a reincarnated Templar. Whether that was the case or not, he was certainly a devotee of a wide range of unusual beliefs, including the Free Energy of Nikola Tesla, and the orgone work of Wilhelm Reich, alongside the furthest-out fringes of the UFO world involving telepathic contact with the Space Brothers and suchlike. In a delightfully genteel and archetypally British development, a series of weird gizmos were constructed to ET specifications including a cosmic coffee pot and some foot warmers. A Star Fellowship was founded with a special badge to extend greetings to the visitors.

In May 1960, Wedd spent some time in the company of Mary Long, an experienced mystic contactee. Following the lead of pioneer theorist Alfred Watkins, Wedd had become particularly interested in clumps of trees on prominent hills as part of the ley network. Long had experienced a bizarre altered state in Wedd's living room where she had apparently seen through the wall to have her attention drawn to an old sycamore tree she felt was somehow important. Overnight she then received a message in her sleep which suggested the tree was the magnetic centre of an alignment that rippled outwards from it across the landscape in the form of a twelve-pointed star. A visit to the tree itself produced further details concerning directions and Wedd was startled to discover that sites he had already investigated were located on the lines. A number of other tree clumps, a spring and a cave were likewise flagged.

Some local UFO sightings indicated the lights in the sky were following paths that included the tree-clump alignments and behaved differently where such lines crossed. This, coupled with clues gleaned from Aime Michell and other UFO literature, led him to surmise that they were using the ley system to navigate.

A short booklet, *Skyways and Landmarks,* was produced on the theme in 1961. It became hugely influential as the decade progressed. The creation of the renowned magazine *The Ley Hunter* was a direct result of its impact. In a letter to the second edition, Brinsley le Poer Trench agreed that *'leys are a most important part of the flying saucer saga'*. A *Ley Hunter's Club* encouraged visits to sites and further investigations.

Interest in UFOlogy in Britain would soon leap from being the concern of a comparative few to the mainstream. Over the August Bank Holiday weekend of 1965 thousands of visitors descended on the normally quiet small Wiltshire town of Warminster following widely publicised UFO activity. The story of the enduring connection of the place with assorted manifestations and the type of questers it attracted is a sociological study in itself that has been excellently covered by the *In Alien Heat* of Steve Dewey and John Ries. There is little doubt that some trickery was present in the early days. The 1965 swarm was not a millennial host of hippie acid heads, although many would soon follow. They were an interesting sample of a wider population, primed with the possibility of response to symbolic stimuli of a certain kind, of things seen in the sky. Despite plenty of hostile depictions in movies, there was a profound attraction rather than fear and the urge to escape.

A RADIANT IMMORTAL IN THE SUMMER OF LOVE

BY THE MID-SIXTIES some aspects of UFOlogy had developed in a manner clearly reflective of the flavour of the time. LSD culture was hugely influenced by it, particularly in Britain, and vice-versa. It seemed to be an inevitable part of the trajectory of any dedicated hallucinogenic voyager that eventually they would encounter in some manner entities, external intelligences, guides etc, who were often experienced as being extra-terrestrial. Tom Wolfe's *Electric Kool-Aid Acid Test* describes such a moment amongst Ken Kesey's pioneering Merry Pranksters. Timothy Leary would eventually become involved in channelling an ET message and advocating space migration. John C. Lilly in *Centre of the Cyclone* provided a map of the territory that included contact with non-human intelligences. It's also clear that staring at the sky under the influence of various drugs makes it more likely that things seen may be mutated to fit the percipients mindset. I can vouch for that personally.

On June 1st 1967 the most legendary of all rock-pop albums, The Beatles *Sgt Pepper,* was released. It does carry a quite extraordinary atmosphere with it that snapshots a stunning period of time and always evokes it. A few weeks later, on June 25th, they represented Britain in an unprecedented satellite TV link-up called *Our World,* performing the specially-composed *All You Need is Love* to an audience estimated at 400 million. It was the peak of the great wave.

July 1st 1967 saw the start of what became one of the most expansive Glastonbury journeys. In *Voyage to Avalon* Robert Coon would later describe himself as '*an immortalist philosopher who has been initiated into all major World Religions and has unified Cabalistic Invocation, ley-line and earth chakra research, and astrology into the Magickal Art of Celestial Alchemy.*' His visionary work has placed the Somerset star temple within a global mystical context, providing a perspective that has been hugely influential in terms of how Glastonbury is seen as a sacred site and an acceptance of the bewildering blend of influences it seems to comfortably accommodate.

Coon is one of many lineal descendants of Mormon founder Joseph Smith, famously visited by an angelic being named Moroni who led him to uncover inscribed tablets. By some mystical process Smith was able to decipher the script and thereby create the *Book of Mormon.* It told the wild tale of the lost tribes of Israel going walkabout and crossing the Atlantic to settle in the Americas. Much scorn has been heaped on Smith and his production but it seems to broadcast across the psychic airwaves in a manner suggestive of a weird truth.

This family heritage proved useful on July 1st 1967, at the peak of the Summer of Love, when Robert Coon was living in Boulder, Colorado. In *Voyage to Avalon* he recalled how, just after midnight, '*a Physically Immortal human from the Realm of Shambhalla instantly and fully materialised within my room. He was not a shimmering vision, but rather a rock solid, Clear human being as real as you or me. This man wore a white robe, held a wooden staff in one hand, had long white hair and beard. He looked incredibly ancient - yet had the radiant Flesh of Eternal Youth.*' This being was none other than the Prophet Elijah, who has apparently also manifested as Merlin, Hermes Trismegistus, and Enoch.

Coon affirmed that this event served to initiate him into the Melchizedek Priesthood. He was also allegedly empowered to reactivate Aleister Crowley's magickal order, the AA (Argenteum Astrum), which he referred to as the Omega Point Foundation.

An enormous cosmic download was communicated that was to be released to the world in astrologically determined stages over the coming decades until 1993. What rapidly developed was a vision of the birth of the Aquarian Age from a location in Southern England. The "global heart chakra" would open there and an "Omega Point" be activated that would lead to the unfolding of the Planetary New Jerusalem and the widespread attainment of physical immortality! Within a few months Robert had narrowed it down to the specific location of Glastonbury, a place that he had never visited. The big event there was scheduled for 1984, 17 years in the future. There was much to be accomplished in the interim.

Robert Coon's work was astrologically determined to an exceptional extent. He attached considerable importance to what he called the Melchizedek cycle. This is a twelve year phase relating to Jupiter that begins with the one year period that the planet is in Aries. In recent years these have been, 1963, 75, 87, 99, and 2011. It would be a major inner cycle in the unfolding of his global magick. He came to believe that his work had been partly set up in 1963 when the Melchizedek immortals, Coon's version of the Secret Chiefs, conferred to set-up three astrologically determined events at Mount Shasta. These triple culminations of Pluto-Uranus in Virgo conjunctions *'activated the New Age movement in California'*.

Some of the details that appeared during the summer of '67 concerned the Aztec calendar. The American poet Tony Shearer had met a mysterious woman in Mexico whilst on a free-floating mystical journey who had introduced him to Quetzalcoatl, the feathered serpent, and the Mesoamerican calendar systems. He looked twenty years ahead to August 1987 as a time of major transformation when the ancient deity would effectively return. Shearer went on to publish a long evocative poem entitled *Lord of the Dawn* on the subject that was initially published in 1971. His communication of these ideas to Jose Arguelles led to the creation of the "New Age Woodstock", the Harmonic Convergence, in 1987. Robert Coon was aware of Shearer's work from the outset and found that it was in complete harmony with his own.

Both men's visions placed great significance on the Tree of Life concept and took inspiration from the same Mexican site. At Santa

Maria del Tule there is a legendary record-breaking Cypress tree that has been adopted as a Mexican national icon. Somewhere between two and three thousand years old and still very much alive and growing, it is believed to be perhaps the oldest and largest living thing on the planet. The gnarled trunk displays shapes that over the years have been interpreted as a variety of animal forms. This has led to it coming to be known as the Tree of Life. Its timescale encompasses the Maya and Aztec civilisations, through the conquest, to the present day. A mythology existed in the area that the historical Toltec era Quetzalcoatl had visited there shortly before his departure westwards into the ocean and promise of return.

The Tree of Life became the centre of Shearer's Quetzalcoatl poetry through which he expressed the calendrical period characterised by thirteen heavens and nine hells leading to a culminating moment in 1987. Robert Coon likewise thought of a return of Quetzalcoatl, envisaging a male dragon force that circles the planet being activated on the same date from El Tule and another major Mexican site, Palenque. He also began working on a thirteen-sphere Enochian Cabala that would later be presented in his book *Voyage to Avalon.*

Robert Coon would not tell his story more widely until the eighties so his ideas concerning Glastonbury stayed under the radar but the place was nonetheless strongly pointed out to the hippie culture during 1967.

THE FLYING SAUCER VISION

'From Glastonbury Tor men left earth to join the Gods'.

The Flying Saucer Vision. John Michell.

JOHN MICHELL'S FIRST BOOK, *The Flying Saucer Vision,* was, as the author later acknowledged, '*a genuine artefact of 1967*'. He had started work on it the previous year, also the time that he had first visited Glastonbury. The *Vision* was a look at the phenomenon throughout history in a manner not dissimilar to Desmond Leslie but now filtered through the perspective of Jung in terms of its re-emergence indicating the profound shift in consciousness that accompanies changing world-ages. Michell recognised the major difficulties of establishing the definitive cause of the UFO phenomenon and advocated the usefulness of observing its effects. It was *'a portent of a further evolutionary step to be brought about through the working of some subtle influence from outside the earth.' 'Flying Saucers may have an entirely physical existence like ours, although using forces of which we are not yet aware. But this seems unlikely in view of their enigmatic behaviour. More probably they belong, like ghosts, to another order of matter. Some aspects of their existence are perceptible to us, for they leave certain physical traces. Moreover the changes which have already taken place due to the psychical effect of their appearance are incalculable.'*

The Bible and other religious texts were investigated with fresh eyes on the look-out for flying saucers and their crews. Michell considered that the motif of the winged disc found in a number of Middle Eastern cultures was a possible symbol of the presence of the UFOnauts.

A classic UFO case involved Brazilian farmer Antonio Vilas-Boas who claimed that he had been taken on board a landed craft in 1957 and introduced to a naked female alien who had sex with him. Michell also examined another two unusual contact cases from the fifties. Howard Menger and Truman Bethurum both regularly encountered female aliens who were physically attractive to them. Michell compared them to the Grail Maidens of Arthurian mythology which implies something of the realm of fairy.

The haunting idea that we may share the world with another race of beings runs throughout *The Flying Saucer Vision.* Fairy lore features an enduring theme of sexual relations between humans and an apparently otherworldly but nonetheless somehow physical race. There are also motifs evocative of abduction cases. Tales tell of dome-shaped mounds with open lighted entrances. Once lured within them, time/space becomes dangerously relative. After partying with the fairy folk, and maybe even having sex with one of them, it would become apparent on leaving that fifty years might have elapsed. Such comparisons open up some of the most fertile ground in UFOlogical research. The early work of Jacques Vallée on this theme gets a mention. The Frenchmen was soon to produce a masterpiece on the subject as we shall see.

Dragon folklore across the world seemed to have points of commonality. Were the flying fire-breathers really alien vehicles? Michell stated that dragons and serpents are interchangeable as motifs of the space deities. The design of the Avebury stone circle supposedly represented a serpent and reverence persisted into the later period of the Druids. Michell's mix leads to the climactic chapter entitled, *The Dragon, the Holy Grail, and the Flying Saucer.* A famous scene in the medieval Arthurian mythology depicts the appearance of the Grail to the knights seated at the round table at Camelot. A bright light filled the hall and a strange object floated overhead attended by an otherworldly maiden. Michell compared this with the famous apparitions of the Virgin Mary at Fatima that climaxed with spectacular aerial effects. He postulated that both are referring to the same UFOlogical phenomenon. Light displays have also been associated with sites of ancient sanctity and it seemed that this would have been a known factor in their placing and whatever activities occurred at them. Is a flying saucer cult the '*basis of all religion*'?

The Trench space opera was not repeated but Michell did ponder in his Grail chapter the possibility that, if the Glastonbury Zodiac could only be fully appreciated from the air, did that mean it was deliberately constructed to perhaps play a part in interaction with extra-terrestrials? Hedging his bets somewhat, he goes on to say that '*Whether or not some great sculpted message to the sky gods does lie below Glastonbury Tor, as Miss Maltwood describes, there is no doubt that the whole area was particularly sacred to the early flying saucer cult.*' Michell mentions the Somerset tale of the Aller dragon. The preponderance of dragon legends in Britain is second only to China. Where dragons coil around hills, that indicates a site sacred to the space gods. Terracing on the Tor may be such dragon coiling. He also seemed to think of the Tor as a sacrificial hill. Whether that means that people were killed there or just abducted is not clearly stated.

1967 also saw the publication of another period-piece, *The Warminster Mystery* by Arthur Shuttlewood, on the apparent spectacular mix of UFO-centred weirdness that had descended on the town. The author was a local journalist who got thoroughly caught up in things, eventually believing himself to be in communication with aliens. He seemed to become the human centre of gravity of the mystery and would later write *UFOs: Key to the New Age.*

Without going into details or deconstruction it is interesting to note that his original book does bring in the subject of leys. Shuttlewood had met Gavin Gibbons, author of two UFOlogical books, in 1965 and was introduced to the whole UFO/ley equation. Gibbons mentioned a unique status for Warminster as twelve leys crossed a point just outside of the town. This might be a factor in what was occurring. Shortly afterwards Shuttlewood received a letter from Jimmy Goddard who was an early associate of Tony Wedd and was involved with Philip Heselton in the *Ley Hunter* magazine that was initially catalysed by *Skyways and Landmarks*. He had been looking into the Warminster ley situation as well and correlating it with some of the UFO sightings. One had happened in the middle of the twelve-ley crossing. *The Warminster Mystery* also mentions a few other local landmarks, mainly churches, stating that they are on leys.

Goddard visited the town in 1966 and participated with Shuttlewood in what became known as a Sky Watch, going away satisfied that he had seen his first UFOs. By then Warminster had become the UK centre for night-time vigils. The locations for these gatherings, which continued for many years, were a group of impressive hills, primarily Cradle Hill but also the enormous Iron Age hillfort, Cley Hill. The proximity of military bases on Salisbury Plain where all manner of activity is occurring around the clock does offer good explanations for many of the lights seen in the sky. Witnesses of the time speak of Shuttlewood clearly misidentifying the planet Jupiter as a UFO and suchlike.

Cley Hill is considered to be part of a number of alignments. Regardless of any of that, it is a most impressive site whose atmosphere after dark would be strongly conducive to unusual experiences. Eventually the most outlandish piece of Warminster lore was associated with it. Keith Palmer, along with Jimmy Goddard, was a member of the International Sky Scouts Association, an organisation founded by Brinsley le Poer Trench. Palmer would claim that in May 1965 a UFO was seen over Warminster that discharged a torpedo-looking object that buried itself in Cley Hill. A long search was instigated involving metal detectors and eventually the incredible artefact was found but left in place. It would be foolish to expect anything remotely resembling evidence of this astounding claim. Shuttlewood also wondered if some kind of homing beacon that served an inscrutable purpose for the UFOnauts might have been buried in one of the great hills thousands of years earlier.

Whilst not as famous a Sky Watch venue as Warminster in 1967, Glastonbury Tor did gain a certain renown amongst hippies as a place to see UFOs and it rapidly became associated with the phenomenon. The timing was perfect as 1967 was a year of what is termed a UFO 'flap' meaning a period of above-average quantity of sightings by people across the whole social spectrum.

John Michell was perhaps the most literate and cultured British contributor to the ever-expanding UFO-centred literature and the timing of his work was perfect for now hippies were let loose in the fields under the night skies of sacred sites and there were no longer any limits to what might unfold. UFOlogy had now fully revitalised the Earth Mysteries. A most peculiar development. The process set in motion by Tony Wedd at the start of the decade went into interstellar overdrive. This was a golden period of good feeling and expansiveness in the subject, at least in Britain. In America, sightings of a winged entity that came to be called Mothman had begun in 1966 and would continue in an area that seemed to be hosting a prolonged UFO season until December 1967 when a terrible bridge collapse ended the saga with loss of life. Researcher John Keel began to have considerable doubts about whatever really lay behind the phenomenon.

The Flying Saucer Vision certainly impacted on Glastonbury itself. *The Central Somerset Gazette* on July 17th 1968 featured an article that wondered '*Was Glastonbury the centre of a Flying Saucer cult in prehistoric times? Is the Tor an ancient sacrificial hill where primitive man placated "the flying gods from the sky?"*' There was a photograph of a mural painted by local artists on a café wall that depicted the Michael ley line passing through the Glastonbury Zodiac with a large winged disc (taken by John Michell as a UFO symbol as we have seen) above it.

1968 saw ancient astronaut theories spread out into popular culture with tremendous vitality. The Stanley Kubrick movie *2001: A Space Odyssey* and the publication in English of Erich von Daniken's *Chariots of the Gods* were followed at the end of the year with the Apollo 8 mission that orbited the moon and provided the now iconic image of Spaceship Earth. Inevitably this led to contemplation of our place in the universe and the obvious thought that if the human race could move into space barely sixty years after first learning the art of flight, who was to say that we may not have been visited ourselves and that the process might be continuing?

* * *

SHAPESHIFTING: MAGONIA AND MARY

IN *The Flying Saucer Vision* there had been mention of fairy lore that seemed to resonate with the UFO mystery, including discussion of strange sexual encounters. The Fatima event was put into a UFO category. The French investigator Jacques Vallée was noted for his early investigations of that evocative cluster of subject-matter. In 1969 he expanded this consideration with *Passport to Magonia*, considered to be a true classic of UFOlogy. Magonia is one of many names for a kind of fairy land, in this case a cloud realm mentioned by a ninth century French bishop from which aerial sailors sallied forth.

Jacques Vallée suggested in *Magonia* that there seems to be one phenomenon which has been interacting with the human race from our earliest days. It takes on different forms in various cultures. He eventually came to believe there is a kind of control system for human consciousness that UFOs may form part of. They may be involved in the manipulation of belief and this makes them very difficult to study. Once again we have to look at the effects that can be attributed to their stimulus.

Vallée demonstrated with numerous examples that the theme of sexual contact between human beings and other non-human species is widespread and ancient. The physical status of these creatures is difficult to determine but they are able to be tangible enough to supposedly mate with us and produce offspring.

Fairy lore has a number of strong motifs. Babies replaced by identical Changelings. Marriages between humans of both sexes and fairy folk. Sometimes they last for a long time until the fairy returns to their home.

Vallée referred to *The Popular Superstitions and Festive Amusements of the Highlanders of Scotland* by William Grant Stewart which includes a chapter called *Of the Passions and Propensities of the Fairies. 'The fairies are remarkable for the amorousness of their dispositions, and are not very backward in forming attachments and connections with the people that cannot with propriety be called their own species.'* W. E. Wentz in his famous study *The Fairy Faith in Celtic Countries* found a living tradition in the early years of the last century and first-hand accounts of continued interaction between the two species. He felt *'that the fairy-women who entice mortals to their love in modern times are much the same, if not the same, as the succubi of middle-age mystics'*.

The incubus and succubus haunted the Catholic medieval world. They were considered to be demonic entities, male and female respectively, encountered in a dream state who entered into sexual congress with the dreamer. There are many accounts suggestive of more than standard dreaming being involved. Vallée discusses at length one seventeenth century case investigated by the prestigious expert philosopher theologian inquisitor Fr Sinistrati. It began when a virtuous married woman eat a pancake of unknown origin. This is itself is redolent of fairy lore. That very night she was disturbed by a voice whispering in her ear. It attempted to seduce her over a period of *'many years'* until her virtue defeated it. A wide range of physical effects that are suggestive of what would now be termed poltergeist cases occurred throughout the woman's ordeal.

The Bible has its famous fragmentary account of *'the Sons of God coming unto the daughters of men'*. The Fallen Angels were capable of mating with human women and producing offspring. They may have taught the arts of civilisation to ancient cultures. Andrew Collins makes a good case in *From the Ashes of Angels* for them being a flesh and blood race but the aura of fear that surrounded the remaining lore that survived into the Middle Ages portrayed them as evil spiritual beings and it was their capacity to breed with humans that defined their threat. The very nature of the Fallen Angels was lustful. Again, a few decades on, the Watchers and Nephilim became associated with aliens via the mythology of Zecharia Sitchin.

John Michell had discussed the Fatima case but Jacques Vallée went into far more detail and investigated the wider topic of Virgin Mary visions in general and their surprising resurgence in modern times.

Fatima is considered to be perhaps the greatest Christian religious manifestation of the twentieth century, at least from a Catholic viewpoint. A group of Portuguese children claimed to have seen and talked to the Virgin Mary. She initially appeared in a globe of light, telling them she would return at monthly intervals, prophesying a spectacular culmination in October. They kept their appointments, accompanied by increasingly large groups of people. Only the children could see her. They were clearly in some kind of trance state. Minor, but odd, external manifestations would weirdly validate their stories. Branches of a tree where the Mary figure was supposed to be hovering bent as if supporting weight, and so on.

The climax saw a huge crowd, approaching a hundred thousand in size, gather for the last appointment. They witnessed a seemingly miraculous heavenly phenomenon. It was as if the sun fell from the sky and plummeted, revolving, with a spectrum of colours towards the earth. Whatever it was that was happening, it was witnessed miles away. Many converted to Catholicism on the spot. It seemed that the woman clothed with the sun from the *Book of Revelation* was tangibly present.

At the very least, a group of small children had been able to assemble a Biblical multitude with exact timing, to witness a spectacular and obviously rare atmospheric event that if it had happened half a century later may well have inspired UFOlogical speculation. That in itself is extremely odd. Looking at other famous cases like Lourdes, it's interesting that the child visionaries at first don't necessarily identify their "contact" as Mary. The response of adults that it obviously must be, conditions what follows. What the being looks like often changes to more fully conform to the archetypal Catholic visuals. Once this is established, messages of the *"I am the Immaculate Conception"* variety follow.

The earlier French case of La Salette in 1846 is another good example of fruitfully comparing the UFOlogical and Catholic realities. Two children saw a globe of light hovering above fields. It opened, disgorging a smaller but brighter light that came down and spoke to them. The Catholic children assumed it must be Our Lady. Prophecies were spoken concerning disease and pestilence which appeared to be validated within a decade. If this had happened in the America of the early nineteen-fifties it seems possible that the light might have taken on the form of the kind of women seen by contactees Howard Menger and Truman Bethuram who John Michell had mentioned.

The modern UFO era has mutated the forms and beliefs of an archetypal mythology to always be just ahead of the current science. In the fifties "aliens" talked of coming from Mars and Venus. Once it was established that those planets couldn't support life, the messages changed. The phenomenon seems to be interactive. We are intimately involved with it. Vallée came to feel that UFOs and their apparent occupants are not necessarily extra-terrestrial.

With Glastonbury we have a location that combines various aspects of the shapeshifting package, fairys, the Virgin Mary, and ultimately, as we shall see, the very landscape itself.

The dedication of the Old Church to the Virgin Mary seems

quite an old one, predating the Mary cult of the Gothic Cathedral era. This probably indicates, more than anything else, that the place, with its rolling hills and springs, was sacred to the divine feminine, although not exclusively so. Does our modern perspective on recent cases allow us to look back and speculate as to whether some numinous luminous manifestation inspired the Mary dedication? Maybe.

Glastonbury has many associations with fairy lore. The best-known of all concerns the Tor itself. Seventh century monk St. Collen, living as a hermit in Glastonbury, was summoned to pay his respects to Gwyn ap Nudd, who is Lord of the Tor, Fairy King and ruler of the underworld known as Annwn. Atop the Tor, Collen somehow entered Gwyn's otherwordly castle where a feast was in progress and music and beauty all around. Not being much of a party person, Collen splashed holy water everywhere and the whole scene disappeared like a mirage. Like most Glastonbury stories its authenticity and even geographical setting are disputed but it has become a permanent part of local folklore. The Tor is considered to be a hollow hill and this is another fairy motif. The validity of associating Gwyn with the Glastonbury landscape has been powerfully affirmed in more recent years by Yuri Leitch in his book *Gwyn*.

The association of Glastonbury with the Isle of Avalon, the paradisiacal land of the dead, is strongly established, essentially indelible, but in many respects quite tenuous. It really began after the alleged discovery of the remains of King Arthur in Glastonbury Abbey. The discovery of the grave seemed to suggest some sort of logic: if Arthur had been laid to rest at Avalon and he'd been found at Glastonbury then it must be Avalon. In this realm he has been healed by the female Merlin, Morgan le Fey, and is capable of one day returning to our world. Such is the mythology that has built up around these fragments. The distinction between a physical Arthur in a grave and an Arthur in a realm between the worlds from whence he can return is unclear. Somehow, in Glastonbury, it is all true.

The Celtic traditions of islands of the dead don't really suggest there was only one of them. The name "Avalon" may well have originally referred to a location other than Glastonbury. What cannot be doubted is that all of the characteristics of Avalon are present in Glastonbury. If it isn't the original one it probably fits the bill even better. We can perhaps recover the details of the place the name derived from. Different theories have been propounded. A good case can be made for Anglesey. Chances are that, unless one is a powerful clairvoyant, such other locations may not feel like a living reality. The new Avalonians would affirm that Glastonbury remains a *functional* Isle of Avalon to this very day and, beyond the sneering of the debunkers, it is that which is of most importance.

The shapeshifting motif extends out into the landscape itself and offers a clue as to what it was that attracted people to Glastonbury in the past. The Tor can be seen from a considerable distance away. It totally dominates the visual field. As one approaches it and circles around it, it presents a different aspect from every vantage point. And yet, there are places in the town where the Tor cannot be seen. The view from its summit is extensive but does not include the Abbey, which is hidden by Chalice Hill, apart from the late addition of the abbot's kitchen. The tower, which is clearly visible from miles away, doesn't really seem that tall when you're inside it. The early inhabitants of Britain led lives far more intimately connected to the land than most people do today. The distinctive qualities of the Glastonbury environs would suggest it was a place of the Otherworld. In those far-off times much of the area was underwater as well. The Tor and its adjoining hills would have been virtually islands. Despite subsequent draining much of the spell remains intact. The whole locale seems to participate in an endlessly shifting perspective.

The same mysterious *something* that can inspire such notions about Arthur and Avalon in the Glastonbury landscape is the same genius loci that can in modern times generate the mutating Temple of the Stars mythos with its ongoing enhancement of effigy designs. By the end of the sixties, it was all fully switched on.

* * *

THE VIEW OVER 1969

THE FOURTH EDITION of the alternative culture hippie magazine *Gandalf's Garden* was published in spring 1969. The editorial wondered *'is 69 is to be the YEAR OF ATLANTIS?'* The first article was entitled *Atlantis Rising* by Mark Western. It began: *'Atlantis is no longer either a fact or a fiction. It has become something greater than both – a hope in man's breast!'* There was also a piece on the Aetherius Society. It was alongside such ideas that a feature on Glastonbury appeared.

Geoffrey Ashe played a major role in the development of modern Glastonbury with his 1957 *King Arthur's Avalon*, a history of the place focusing on the Abbey. It was not a wildly mystical work but was sufficient to encourage a growing tide of pilgrims. He lived in a house at the foot of the Tor once occupied by Dion Fortune. A Catholic and by no means a hippie, he nonetheless had a free-ranging mind partly inspired by William Blake and recognised that the sixties youthquake, which accommodated enthusiasm for Arthurian topics in general as well as Glastonbury was important. In 1967 he had been secretary of the archaeological dig at Cadbury Castle, associated with Camelot, not far from Glastonbury. This would later inspire his 1971 masterpiece *Camelot and the Vision of Albion*. In 1969 he contributed a short article to *Gandalf's Garden* entitled *Glastonbury: Key to the Future*. Ashe said that

> *'Britain will begin to be reborn when Glastonbury is. The Giant Albion will begin to awake when his sons and daughters gather inside the enchanted boundary, and summon him with the right words, the right actions, a different life.'*

Also featured in the magazine was *The Glastonbury Giants (Somerset's Secret Zodiac)* by Mary Caine. The basic corpus that would form her life's work was already in place. Readers of her books would recognise all of the essential elements in this early presentation, which included a number of illustrations.

Caine had joined the London Order of Druids in 1961. It was in such company that she first heard of the Glastonbury Zodiac. Initially sceptical, she decided to write to Katharine Maltwood in Canada with detailed questions. She received a reply from her husband stating that his wife had died just three months before. It was at the same time that Caine had first heard of her work. There was a sense of synchronicity. Mary came to feel that in that period of time, the work was in some sense handed over to her to carry on. It's intriguing to remember that during the same period Brinsley le Poer Trench was also corresponding with John Maltwood whilst preparing *Men Among Mankind*.

Caine made adjustments to some of Maltwood's figures and even added new ones of her own. The most famous aspect of her work was the noticing through aerial photography of what appeared to be a conventional depiction of the face of Christ on the summit of a hill fort called Dundon Beacon. The fact that it happened to lie over the exact area already identified as the head of the Gemini figure rendered it all the more peculiar. It became the most widely distributed image connected with the Glastonbury Zodiac and was shown on BBC TV. Mary Caine was inevitably drawn to refer to Blake's question, '*did the countenance divine shine forth upon our clouded hills*'? It was also notable that the very peak of the hill, where beacon fires had once been lit, was the area on the effigy's head where the yogic third eye was situated. The name of the Druidic bard Taliesin meant "radiant brow" and this seemed to fit the general mythic mix of the Gemini figure very well. Unfortunately, during the nineties, the trees were cleared and the Christ simulacra no longer exists.

Mary Caine would become the greatest champion of the landscape temple over a period of decades. Her cryptic allusive poetic style would deter academics and entice potential landscape mystics.

Indubitably the greatest of all Earth Mysteries works, John Michell's *The View Over Atlantis,* was published in 1969, achieving instant cult classic status. It presented a comprehensive survey of a widely varied field and permeated the whole of hippiedom. Various notions that had previously been held only by obscure eccentrics now reached thousands of impressionable minds. Having already covered the UFOlogical field, Michell steered generally clear of it but the work of Katharine Maltwood was again featured.

Alfred Watkins ley work was presented in detail. Michell then went on to look at other cultures with fresh eyes. He provided a supremely eloquent, poetic vision of what these studies seemed to suggest.

Australian aboriginal spirituality provided fertile ground for comparison and stimulation. Their mythology told of a primordial period of creation known as the dreamtime, when the landscape was brought into its current form by the activities of divine beings whose deeds formed the eternal exemplary models for human behaviour. Paths across the land called songlines connected sacred sites. At certain times in the calendar it was necessary to walk these lines to revitalise them and ensure their proper alignment to the forces of creation by singing the very songs by which the world had been brought into being.

Ancient China yielded fine fruit in the form of the art of Feng Shui. The Chinese had a complex culture concerning the land as a living entity that needed to be related to in a state of harmony. To this end, buildings were sited in accordance with precise laws. The energy of the life-force, symbolised as a dragon, moved in channels through the land and ebbed and flowed depending on the nature of the terrain, whether mountain and valley and so on. Subtle procedures could aid and enhance its beneficial effects in an individual home and in the larger design of towns and cities. A wrongly placed building could bring misfortune and ill health to occupants. The art is still in use in the present day and can therefore be investigated in great detail.

All over the world, traditional societies had a way of interacting with their locale that had many points in common. In the light of these cross-cultural studies, it seemed valid to look at British legendary traditions and prehistory in a similar way to look for indications of the same kind of patterns. An exciting picture was revealed. The megalithic stone circle at Avebury had been considered by the eighteenth century antiquarian William Stukely to be a serpent temple of the Druids. We now know it considerably predates them but the serpent idea seems to gel with the Chinese concepts. Moving on from his earlier association of the serpent with UFOs, Michell also suggested that the serpent perhaps symbolised the life energy in the ground. Alfred Watkins had originally felt that the leys were practical means of navigation. In later life he began to acknowledge the possibility that they had more esoteric purposes. John Michell affirmed that they marked paths of earth energy. It seemed the megalithic builders had a way of understanding this force and perhaps the ley system served a similar function to the Chinese Feng Shui arts. Dowsers are a modern example of people who appear to be sensitive to invisible forces beneath the ground, whether it be water, magnetic currents, or something more unclassifiable. Such sensitives have always existed and it seems likely the megalithic people could have made use of them.

Michell looked again at British folklore concerning dragons and moved beyond his initial UFO associations. The English patron saint, George, is of course the most famous of dragon killers, closely followed by the Archangel St. Michael. It is interesting to see how many churches dedicated to Michael are situated on hilltops. Glastonbury Tor is the obvious example. One of John Michell's most important and enduring visionary insights was to notice an apparent alignment of Michael churches across the south of England. This has become probably the world's most famous ley line. It stretches from St. Michael's Mount in Cornwall, through his churches at Brentor, Burrow Mump in Somerset and the Tor, and goes on through Avebury stone circle and into Norfolk and the abbey at Bury St. Edmunds. It travels across the longest continuous stretch of land in southern England. Many more churches dedicated to St. Michael fall upon it.

The suggestion is that the dragon force in the landscape was recognised by early Christians and certain esoterically-inclined church builders of the early Middle Ages. It became equated in the popular mind with the Devil. Michael was considered to be the ideal figure to keep these forces in check, due to his role in the *Book of Revelation* "War in Heaven". The real nature of Michael's relationship to the dragon force and what he himself may truly represent is an ongoing study. The original formulation of the line has set countless pilgrims off along it. It is now officially marked on a National Trust direction-finding plinth on the summit of Glastonbury Tor as the "dragon path".

The second part of Michell's book claimed to reveal a cosmology of sacred geometry and mathematical mysticism that the creators of these ancient edifices, from Stonehenge to Glastonbury Abbey, and even Egypt's Great Pyramid, had in common. The suggestion is that they all may have been heirs to knowledge that was a relic of some unknown previous culture, generally thought of as "Atlantis". This canon of thought has formed a major part of the wisdom tradition of humanity, supposedly being passed down through the ages by the likes of Pythagoras and Plato, the Masons, the builders of the Gothic cathedrals and so on. Music has been an integral part of it, as its laws are believed to show how the harmony of creation functions. Even if one is not mathematically minded it can be an intoxicating experience to try and follow Michell's elucidation of these ideas.

The most evocative of all the Glastonbury material in the book is the suggestion that the geometrical plan that its Abbey was constructed upon was deliberately intended to duplicate the pattern of the city of the New Jerusalem in the *Book of Revelation*. A similar geometry may, perhaps, be found in the layout of Stonehenge. The plan predates Christianity and represents an ideal of harmony that brings together the laws of heaven and earth through the geometrical forms of divine creation. Glastonbury Abbey was considered to be the successor to Stonehenge in a new epoch. That this is so is not only suggested by the geometrical grid-plan but also by the existence of an apparent ley alignment that travels right up the centre of the Abbey and the aptly-named Dod Lane just outside it, to Stonehenge. The complex unfolding of the geometry and the Stonehenge, Glastonbury, Egypt connection, was further elaborated in Michell's next book, *City Of Revelation* (later revised as *The Dimensions of Paradise*).

One further idea that has become a major part of the modern Glastonbury blend also fully surfaced in 1969, in time to be assimilated into some remarkable speculations that would soon follow. One of the most notable visual aspects of Glastonbury Tor is the terracing on its slopes. On a sunny day it can be distinctly delineated by the play of light and shadow. A generally held theory contends that it derives solely from medieval agricultural practices. In recent times others have come to feel differently. We have noted the Atlantean speculations of Dion Fortune.

In 1944, Geoffrey Russell had a mystical experience in Ceylon. In struggling to understand its meaning he produced a drawing of a pattern featuring various circles. He felt that it was something to do with the human brain. Nearly twenty years later he saw a picture of a sevenfold labyrinthine maze design that had been discovered on a rock face near Tintagel and was considered by some to be perhaps three-thousand years old. He was stunned to recognise essentially the same design that he had drawn. This inspired him to undertake a study of the topic from both a historical and psychological perspective.

Mazes are most famously associated with Crete and the tale of the Minotaur. A particular maze pattern, known as "Cretan" and septenary in form, of which the Tintagel case is one example, can be found in many places around the world.

The most striking result of Geoffrey Russell's journey of discovery was his theory that the Tor terracing is a unique three-dimensional form of the Cretan septenary maze design. Russell linked his postulated Tor maze to a famous Welsh Dark Age tale, *The Spoils of Annwn.* It's an early story of Arthur in which he and his companions go in search of a wonder-working cauldron that seems to be a precursor of the medieval Grail. One of the featured locations is Caer Sidi. This is taken to mean the turning or spiral castle. Russell believes this motif shows a memory of maze-threading ceremonials. Somewhere in this mystery, the secret of the Grail waits to be revealed.

A 1969 anthology, *Glastonbury: a Study in Patterns,* featured an article by Russell on his theory. It was perfect timing with so many other elements of the total modern mythos coming together.

Geoffrey Russell never attempted what seems the obvious way to validate his theories. He never tried to actually walk the maze. It would be ten years before Geoffrey Ashe successfully took up the challenge and helped set in motion many a traversal of the labyrinth. How does this fit in, if at all, with the Tor as part of Aquarian Phoenix idea? Are they mutually exclusive? At least one solution has been put forward.

THE STARMAN AND A FREE FESTIVAL

IN JULY 1969, nine days before the moon landing, David Bowie released his song *Space Oddity.* It was well-timed and gave him an immediate huge success. It would however be a few years before he fully established himself as rock god. During that time he lived in a large flat in a Gothic Victorian villa in Beckenham in South London. It was there that he wrote the three classic albums, *The Man Who Sold the World, Hunky Dory* and *Ziggy Stardust.* His interests and behaviour during that period provide an intriguing glimpse into late sixties psychedelic UFOlogy.

The place served as a free-form sex, drugs and weirdness den. On the day of the moon landing, Bowie supposedly saw a spacecraft land in the road. One night he attempted to communicate with aliens by standing on the roof and holding a wire coat-hanger up to the sky and only stopped when someone on the ground shouted up a humorous remark at him.

It does seem, from fragments in later interviews, that Bowie had a considerable interest in the subject. He mentioned being associated with two men who published a British UFO magazine and experiencing multiple light-in-the-sky sightings every night for about a year. '*We had regular cruises that came over. We knew the 6.15 was coming in and would meet up with another one. And they would be stationary for about half an hour, and then after verifying what they'd been doing that day, they'd shoot off.*' (from *Creem* magazine in Feb 1975). It has to be said that this does rather sound like the straightforward activity of aeroplanes.

In 1969 Bowie had been performing at a Folk Club in a back room of a Beckenham pub then called *The Three Tuns*. He helped create an *Arts Lab* there where the performances were a bit more experimental. The group soon organised an outdoor Free Festival on the Beckenham Croydon Road Recreation Ground on 16th August, the same weekend that the Woodstock festival was happening. Compared to the 400,000 of the American event, 3,000 was a modest attendance.

In September, he wrote and recorded *Memory of a Free Festival* in commemoration. The depiction of a loved-up tripped out crowd of hippies in a field experiencing a timeless afternoon permeated by flying saucer religion has long been a particular favourite of mine in providing a permanent snapshot of the feel of an era as effective as anything on *Sgt Pepper*. The song can be found on the album now known as *Space Oddity*. It seems a plaintive lament for an innocence already lost.

'It was ragged and naïve, it was Heaven.'
'I kissed a lot of people that day.'
'Someone passed some bliss among the crowd.'
'We scanned the skies with rainbow eyes and
saw machines of every shape and size.'
'We talked with tall Venusians passing through.'

After a hubbub of strange noises the song changes into a long anthemic chorus clearly inspired by The Beatles *Hey Jude* but expressing somewhat different sentiments.

'The sun-machine is coming down and we're gonna have a party.'

It is fitting that Bowie's next big hit was the obviously ET-themed *Starman*. Following his legendary performance of it on the BBC *Top of the Pops* programme in 1972 in exotic attire his personal star ascended spectacularly.

* * *

ANTHONY ROBERTS: SOWER OF THUNDER

WE HAVE SEEN how many expressions of the emerging Glastonbury zeitgeist surfaced in 1969. Anthony Roberts became the centre of another vital part of the total mix but one that has remained unknown until now. The mid-seventies *Glastonbury: Ancient Avalon, New Jerusalem* anthology would be the high-water mark of acceptance of the landscape zodiac idea. It contains only the briefest of references to the subject of UFOs but the fundamental experience of the inner life of its editor, without which the anthology would probably never have existed, was a mysterious sighting of something profoundly unidentified in 1969.

Anthony Roberts was born on May 4th 1940, within days of the start of the German invasion of France that would lead to Dunkirk and the Battle of Britain. He came to the Avalonian mythos from a background of anarchistic activism. As an advocate of the CND cause he broke into an American airbase as far back as 1963 in an attempt to disable some of the planes. He and his wife Janet met through campaigning against the imprisonment of Nelson Mandela. He was repeatedly arrested at political protests and attained maximum street credibility by starting a fire in the foyer of the Dorchester Hotel as a statement against capitalism. As a young man he corresponded with J. R. R. Tolkien. Working as a librarian at the London *Evening News* and then *The Times* allowed him the freedom to become an autodidactic polymath. He developed a mystical conviction of the eternal true nature of the spiritual tradition of Britain as best exemplified by William Blake.

Reading Geoffrey Ashe's *King Arthur's Avalon* as a teenager in 1959 had introduced him to Glastonbury. He first visited the place in 1965. In 1967, John Michell's *The Flying Saucer Vision* opened him up to the UFOlogical Earth Mysteries connection and most importantly of all, the Glastonbury Zodiac. The Roberts spent quite a bit of time around Glastonbury in the late sixties during the time of the arrival of the early hippie pilgrims and more sober mystics. They hung out in the café with the Michael line Zodiac mural, meeting John Michell and a number of other interesting people.

It was shortly after the climactic event of the decade in the summer of 1969, the moon landing, and the time of David Bowie's Free Festival, that Anthony and Janet Roberts were to have the defining experience of their lives. It would happen not that far away from Bowie's rooftop coat-hanger signalling. Remembering John Michell's advice concerning the difficulties involved in establishing the definitive cause of the UFO phenomenon and the usefulness of observing its effects will be a valuable perspective to maintain.

> *'While driving with my wife one evening during the Autumn of 1969, we were shown both a vision and a sign in the sky. We were driving South out of London towards Dorking and had reached the Tolworth round-about on the Kingston-by-pass. It was not quite dark, the air was very clear, and there was as yet no trace of the moon. At the same time both my wife and I saw a huge, white disc shining in the sky in the middle distance ahead of us. It was about the size of a very large grapefruit and as we slowed down to watch, its colour changed slightly to silvery gold with faint tinges of orange fire playing around the extreme edges. We slowed our car still more, and as we watched we saw a string of small, glowing discs appear on the left hand side of the larger one; they flickered and twinkled with a pearly and opalescent glow, faintly mauve and very beautiful. After lining up in a perfectly straight formation, they gradually merged one by one into the larger disc.*
>
> *Whatever it was, suddenly, with tremendous speed and in complete silence, the huge object moved from in front of our car to behind it in a matter of seconds. We quickly stopped and got out. It now hung motionless in the distance and as we looked up at it, a terrific feeling of peace, physical lightness and spiritual happiness came over us, leaving us deeply moved. The strange aeriel object next began moving very swiftly towards us, pulsating faintly, with a green light blazing on one side and a blue light on the other. It stopped again and hovered low in the sky to the north-east, then began to move slowly, quartering the air in precise, sweepingly geometrical lines, rather like a fish darting through water. It was tracing a definite star pattern in the sky which had now become dark, and as we stared in wonder, it yet again stopped and hung like an exquisite, glowing jewel above us. Then suddenly it was gone! With unbelievable acceleration it shot upwards into space and vanished into the now starry night. The whole sighting had lasted about 20 minutes and yet it felt as though we had been watching for hours.'*

Janet later recalled in the memorial booklet, *From Atlantis to Avalon*, how '*we sat and cried*'. '*For me it felt as though I had glimpsed God in action – although this was a mechanical activity. I was moved as though I had a religious experience.'*

Something of the mixed blessings of such close encounters manifested only a few days later when Tony was knocked off his scooter by a car. The injuries sustained required six months off work but enabled him to undertake a marathon reading and writing stint, fired-up by his revelatory experience.

A manuscript of 300 large pages, a work of *'historical synthesis and speculative imagination'*, provisionally entitled *Giants in the Earth* (from which the above account was taken), resulted during the next year. It was a wild mix firmly based on the existence of Mu and Atlantis. The lost continents were featured in considerable detail. Roberts was a passionate devotee of fantasy literature and used something of its novelistic format to convey the density of detail he had amassed from a variety of sources. Mu was in fact a topic that had featured in his inner life for some time. Radiant fifteen-foot-tall aliens walked the earth amongst us. After Mu was destroyed following a comet strike, they helped in the establishment of Atlantis.

After beginning with the lost continents, the second part of *Giants* was entitled *The Colonies of Atlantis* and dealt with Egypt, Britain, and the Americas. Projected further chapters on China, India, and Africa were never written. The ideas of Brinsley le Poer Trench were strongly present, in long quotes, and most importantly, the belief that the Glastonbury Zodiac is the work of Atlanteans. They initially arrived in Britain 20,000 years ago, when the settlements founded in the times of Mu had long disappeared. Their presence was strongest in Ireland, Cornwall, and Somerset. British folklore is full of references to dragons, giants, faeries, inundations, and powerful races of magical beings from the sea. All of these contain Atlantean elements. As Roberts would later say in *Sowers of Thunder*, *'Behind every megalithic stone there looms the shadow of a giant. Behind every giant there shines the imagery of a transcendent culture of divinely inspired beings'*.

In its global survey *Giants* built on the work of Leslie and Trench, featuring the vimanas, along with dramatic statements concerning the Great Pyramid having been built *'by the magical powers of the Atlantean Adepts and the Giants in 15,000BC'* using *'levitation, telekinesis, and vibrational manipulation of sound'*. The Sphinx is even older.

In a passage that perhaps now seems very much of its time, Roberts stated that *'The modern alchemical student who ingests "acid" and departs on a beautiful, spiritual voyage of revelation and discovery, is in a direct line of descent from the Atlantean adepts of the past'*.

Looking at the manuscript in 2013, it seemed to me to lie somewhere halfway between *Morning of the Magicians* and Graham Hancock's *Fingerprints of the Gods*, certainly a triumph of fantastic realism but filled with enough historical data to give pause for thought. Although unfinished in terms of its original conception, Roberts' first book *Atlantean Traditions in Ancient Britain*, featuring an extensive treatment of the Glastonbury Zodiac, would later be extracted from it almost verbatim. *Sowers of Thunder* was also mined from the mother lode.

I find it intriguing to contemplate a timeline in which *Giants in the Earth* was finished and published round about 1971, taking its place alongside a whole bunch of other ancient astronaut works. Our perceptions of that period in Glastonbury would surely change to some extent. Alongside the 1969 brew that tangibly developed into the way the town was perceived in the seventies, the extent of UFOlogical inspiration, primarily in connection with the terrestrial zodiac would be far clearer. Published or not, the contents and their initial inspiration are still part of that incredible 1969 mix and they do demonstrate quite clearly how much Earth Mysteries UFOlogy was part of Glastonbury's total character at that time.

During the period of writing, the Roberts had another strange experience with mysterious lights, this time on Glastonbury Tor. The owner of the mural café was another visionary. Gino Gennaro would eventually write in 1979 one of the strangest of all Glastonbury works, *The Phenomena of Avalon, The Story of this Planet as Recounted by the Fairies.* He underwent a kind of Jacques Vallée process encountering Venusians/fairies on the holy hill and received a Gnostic Hermetic teaching he illustrated with artwork by William Blake. The combination of the two visionaries and the Tor produced etheric fireworks one sunny afternoon when Tony and Jan Roberts were with Gino and his wife Nancy on the slopes. Spheres of light appeared to arise from the earth and float around.

Such light manifestations around the Tor itself rather than in the skies above it were not uncommon during that broad period of the late sixties and early seventies. Long-term resident Bern Chandler recalled how one evening at dusk *'I glanced up at the Tor and there was a sudden rush of gold light, similar to that on a gold rimmed cloud at sunset, but it had an amazing energy about it. It wasn't just glowing round the tower, it was like a welding torch but yellow/gold! and without any sound. Most unexpected. It lasted for maybe 15-20 seconds in my consciousness, then faded as if its power supply was gradually being turned off.'*

The 1971 Glastonbury music festival was a major event for the town. The tide of alternative culture types who made their way to the town and ultimately settled there increased in intensity from that time onwards. Captured for posterity in the movie *Glastonbury Fayre,* it was the first of the epic gatherings that are now as much a part of the British social calendar as Wimbledon and the FA Cup final. The famous pyramid stage was placed through dowsing and the advice of John Michell. The mysticism of the time was hanging heavily in the airwaves. A measure of that comes from an experience of Jan Roberts on Glastonbury Tor one afternoon whilst the festival was occurring. She and Tony were looking in the direction of the site when she briefly saw, rising from the landscape, made from the very earth itself, the titanic form of the Glastonbury Zodiac Sagittarius Arthur figure. It marked a mythic moment in time. A vision of a true giant in the earth, rising as the modern Glastonbury was coming into being and nicely completing the period of the enormous burst of creativity begun in 1969.

Anthony Roberts became one of the most charismatic figures in the field. Mary Caine saw him as, '*a returned Atlantean, an ancient Briton, a Druid*'. He expressed passionate prophetic raptures and rages, unafraid of any controversies and consequences. As a result of this personal style, he attracted and repelled people in equal proportions.

THE OMEGA POINT & THE EMBRYOGENESIS OF THE WORLD SENSORIUM

IN JANUARY 1971 Robert Coon publicly proclaimed that Glastonbury is planetary heart chakra and that the global Omega Point would be activated at Easter sunrise 1984 atop the Tor along with a female dragon energy, complementary to the male, that likewise circles the world.

On Christmas Day 1973, as Comet Kohoutek passed behind the sun, Robert has said he had his only meeting with Melchizedek. The instructions he received began his great global chakra work with the '*Shasta-Great Pyramid-Glastonbury formula*'. This was '*opening the Heart of Gaia so that the feminine Rainbow Serpent current could flow without restriction around the world.*'

Robert Coon was not the only person pondering the Omega Point during the early seventies. Some background to the concept is useful. Teilhard de Chardin was probably the most influential and extraordinary Catholic thinker of the twentieth century. His ideas brought him into repeated conflict with the Vatican. In *The Phenomenon of Man* Teilhard postulated a further strata of the life of the planet above the biosphere that he called the *noosphere*, the "thinking layer". The collective mindstuff of expanding humanity is creating an ever more powerful field of consciousness around the planet. It seems that, '*evolution is an ascent towards consciousness — therefore it should culminate forwards in some sort of supreme consciousness*'. Every consciousness can centre everything partially upon itself, can centre itself upon itself and is '*being brought more by this very super-centration into association with all the other centres surrounding it.*' '*Because it contains and engenders consciousness, space-time is necessarily of a convergent nature. Accordingly it's enormous layers, followed in the right direction, must somewhere ahead become involuted to a point which we might call Omega, which fuses and consumes them integrally in itself.*'

If the Vatican didn't rush to embrace these expansive ideas, there were many that did. They seemed to express something generally present in the zeitgeist airwaves.

Oliver Reiser was a Professor in the Philosophy department at Pittsburgh University for fifty years. He wrote a book on the Glastonbury Zodiac entitled *This Holyest Erthe* that was published in 1974. I can't really imagine a British philosopher producing a book on such a subject that mentioned Atlantis and quoted Blavatsky as an authority. A lot of the so-called history in the book could be considered a bit dubious. It's only a short work but perhaps takes the Zodiac corpus to its most extreme and extraordinary expression in a way that enhances appreciation of the potential significance of the Omega Point.

Thanks to Lovelock's Gaia hypothesis it's no longer thought to be wildly eccentric to believe that our planet can be considered to be a living organism. Ecological studies have increasingly shown the awesome level of interconnectedness of all the many systems that function in the world. Many have found the contemplation of this interconnectedness to be a doorway to a form of mysticism.

What function do human beings serve in the midst of all this? Our consciousness is the most specialised yet seen here. Are we in effect part of a bigger picture of the planet evolving, coming to consciousness of itself and its place in the Universe? Is our apparent individuality, our separation, an illusion? Are we somehow the cells of a global brain? Reiser was speculating along these lines quite a while before the New Agers took it on board. He'd been influenced by Teilhard de Chardin. He also tried to see the unfolding of the history of human cultures within the frame of that bigger picture.

Here's a condensed sample of Reiser's mind at work. It's worth reading over it a few times.

> *'For a complete theory of any complex social phenomenon one requires a full-blown philosophy of history and theory of man.... This will be a non-linear and wholistic interpretation. In that more complete statement two facets will receive further elaboration: (1) there will be an organismic theory of the earth as a living entity, with human society as a part of that evolving creature; and (2) there will be a theory of the origin of human consciousness in terms of its bi-polar sources in (1) the human nervous system, and (2) the radiation belt (or psi field), the two poles generating the "world sensorium"- the guiding field which controls the psychosocial evolution of mankind.*
>
> *'On the side of the earth organism, we have long argued the case for the doctrine of the evolution of a giant earth-creature, the idea that the earth is indeed a living being, with the plant and animal kingdoms forming (functionally) the entoderm and ectoderm of the giant earth-egg, with the human race constituting the maturing nervous system of the embryo and individual persons serving as the "neuroblasts" of the creature. We have urged that the eastern and western hemispheres are analagous to the right and left lobes of the human brain, together constituting the armature of an earth dynamo spinning out the lines of force ("wires") of the coming electromagnetic society.*
>
> *'Accordingly the planetary cortex of the electromagnetic society gives rise to its radiation-belt "elecroencephalograms." These are the lines of force of the psi-field that are associated in cause-effect relations (feed-back) with the two halves of the earth-armature and the subordinate ganglia of the global cogitatorium. The evolving system of life is operated by the energy of the sun (as the ancient Druids knew), which elaborates the essential substances (e.g., chlorophyll) that the earth-egg requires.*
>
> *'The human beings (neuroblasts) of the differentiating forebrain are not yet the perfect neurons they will later come to be. This, of course, implies that human history, the rise and fall of nations, the migrations of peoples, cultural diffusions, and the rest, are phases of*

the rhythmic pulsations of the planetary electroencephalograms, playing like electric signs over a bank of lights.

'We hold that consciousness is a manifestation of a feed-back polarity between the human cortex and the environing "radiation belts" of a "world sensorium," this latter being our substitute for the Noosphere of Teilhard de Chardin. These postulated fields - or psi-belts - have their "magnetic moments"...synchronicities between levels or planes of action-patterns, which are the secular-historical events occurring over the surface of the earth and reflecting a kind of electromagnetic induction. The field-aspects constitute the akashic records which provide the prototypes that may constitute the morphogenetic images in the various eras of human endeavour and achievement.'

Reiser pondered on the Aquarian phoenix, trying to divine its possible message for the emerging age. A problem seems to appear. '*How is it possible, at one and the same time, for the Tor Hill to be Mrs. Maltwood's "Phoenix" and Mr. Russell's "labyrinth"?*' The resolution is contained in perhaps the most far-out single sentence ever penned on the mystery of Glastonbury. '*Is it possible that the labyrinth will turn out to be the morphogenetic field pattern for the embryogenesis of the World Sensorium?*' What does that mean?

Reiser believed that human awareness cannot be separated from the radiation belts of the World Sensorium, the global brain. This brain uses us to become conscious of itself. The whole process unfolds through mathematical laws, geometric forms. The Tor maze may model a brain pattern. It could be a place where the World Sensorium expresses itself in a manner that brings humans into an increased accelerated relationship with itself. They may become consciously attuned to it. Any form of interaction at all helps the process along. The maze could be seen as the brain of the Aquarian phoenix. The consciousness attainable through it represents the blueprint, the morphogenetic field pattern, the shape of the coming epoch. It has lain comparatively dormant but now is the time of its activation. The embryogenesis of the World Sensorium, the coming to birth and maturity of the planet's consciousness can be crucially affected by whether or not the Aquarian phoenix is able to fulfil its total potential function.

⋆ ⋆ ⋆

INVOCATION

THE MOST WELL-KNOWN and influential New Age prayer is probably Alice Bailey's *Great Invocation*, part of the gigantic corpus of work supposedly dictated to her by the inner plane contact Djwhal Khul. It begins,

'From the point of Light within the Mind of God
Let light stream forth into the minds of men.'

Widely used throughout the New Age movement, it has, for example, been publicly recited in Glastonbury at the time of the full moon regularly since the seventies. The Findhorn Foundation give it considerable status

Robert Coon believed he had composed a replacement and the circumstances are of considerable interest and relevance to his Glastonbury work. On September 5th 1975, during one of the Melchizedek Cycle years, he was at Excalibur Hill on Mount Tamalpeis near San Francisco, a location he considered to be energetically linked to Shasta. It was the new moon in Virgo and the day of the Jewish New Year. A group of light spheres appeared to him that he believed were manifestations of immortal beings from the Jewish lineage including Enoch, Melchizedek, Elijah, and Moses. They stayed with him for an hour and did all kinds of strange stuff on his inner being.

The ministrations of each light being in turn resulted in one line of the new *Invocation of the Omega Point* being produced. Coon did not believe it was a kind of telepathic transmission but a product of his own attuned higher consciousness. The final thirteen lines equalled Bailey's original.

'Know, Oh Universe, that I Love You
With All the Grace, and with All the Power, of the Love of Messiah...
That my awareness is Eternally caressing all Forms of Reality,
Sharing this Bliss in the most Beautiful and Creative Manifestations...

Let my Heart be possessed by the Spirit of Truth! Let my
Existence be Dedicated to the enlightenment of All Consciousness
Throughout the Universe! Let my Enthusiasm be a Light of Love
and Truth for all to Feel! Oh Let my Touch be the Highest
Manifestation for the Will Divine!

*

Let my every Action transform this Reality into Greater and More Loving Perfections! Let my Body be the Most Sacred Temple Of Truth! The Omega Point is Here! Clarity of Vision Has been Redeemed throughout the Universe!'

Robert Coon believed that his poem was due to spiritually supersede Bailey's during the centenary of the Theosophical Society the following month. This event served as the midway point in the process leading from the July 1967 download to the Glastonbury Omega Point in 1984 which was to specifically feature the use of the *Invocation.*

The so-called Melchizedek Cycle years do not exactly coincide with the Gregorian calendar year. The *Invocation* was received in a year running between March 1975 and March 1976. Towards the end of that cycle, during the time of the appearance of Comet West, Coon was in El Tule burying a ruby and an emerald magickally set to activate eleven years later at the moment of sunrise on August 17th 1987.

ANCIENT AVALON, NEW JERUSALEM

1977 WAS A DAMN STRANGE YEAR in Britain. Remembered in popular culture for punk rock, there were a lot of echoes of 1967 flowing through it as well. The two years shared an above-average number of UFO reports and it seems in retrospect that there was almost a final flourishing of books and artefacts of popular culture that carried the sixties inspiration.

Stephen Jenkins' *The Undiscovered Country* combined serious ley hunting, the full spectrum of UFOlogical and paranormal weirdness, and the incredible suggestion by its Mongolian Kalachakra initiate author that Glastonbury may be the fabled Shambhala. Geoffrey Ashe's *Ancient Wisdom* also examined the possibility of an archaic cultural link between Glastonbury and Central Asia. The charming *Shambhala* by Andrew Tomas covered common ground and wove in ET lore. In the USA, Robert Anton Wilson's *Cosmic Trigger: Final Secret of the Illuminati,* an intoxicating consciousness expanding smorgasbord of sixties lore infused with psychedelia, UFOlogy, the mysteries of the Kennedy assassination, secret society paranoia, all-round strangeness, and featuring such luminaries as

Timothy Leary and Aleister Crowley, appeared.

Hippie guitar legend Steve Hillage produced his album *Motivation Radio* featuring UFOs on the cover and tracks entitled *Saucer Surfing* and *Light in the Sky*, which included the lyrics

'We're picking up the pieces of the puzzle of the saucer machines,
we've seen every crazy story all rolled into one and
now we see just what it means'.
'In seventy seven the light shone from our hearts and from our eyes,
we looked into the ethers and we saw that they were very much alive'.

It was the year of the greatest of all UFOlogical movies, *Close Encounters of the Third Kind,* (although it didn't appear in British cinemas until early the following year). Avebury stone circle was memorably featured in the British cult masterpiece of kiddies TV, *Children of the Stones,* with its Earth Mysteries literate script.

However much some of it all may now seem out of date or just plain wrong, one could do a lot worse than grab the whole lot and feast on it for a few months. It provides a further sense of context for the Glastonbury anthology.

Glastonbury: Ancient Avalon, New Jerusalem was conceived and created in London. The first edition was published in 1976 by the Roberts themselves in their Zodiac House imprint. It was a compilation of articles with Anthony Roberts as editor, featuring twelve pieces as a deliberate resonance with the tale of the legendary twelve hides of land given to Joseph of Arimathea that is the basis of so much Glastonbury lore, and the twelve signs of the landscape zodiac.

The anthology featured a long article by Mary Caine, repeating her basic Zodiac theories in sign by sign detail. She was fresh from some considerable success. The BBC had made a short film with her for the popular early evening news programme *Nationwide* that was screened in 1976. Mary Caine's most complete expression of the subject, the "big green book", *The Glastonbury Zodiac: Key to the Mysteries of Britain,* was published in 1978 and remains the most successful work on the subject.

An article by Jan Roberts spoke of further landscape figures she felt she had discovered in the Glastonbury environs, the Polden Hound and Aller Dragon. Other contributions dealt with the possible existence of more British terrestrial zodiacs. The evocative subject of underground tunnels was raised. The item most likely to be considered downright eccentric came from American Donald L. Cyr who favoured an ice crystal canopy theory suggestive of a huge reflective cloud, similar to one discovered on Venus, which would enable the landscape effigies to be seen from the ground.

It was entirely appropriate that the last article in the anthology came from John Michell, Anthony Roberts' great friend and the person most responsible for the modern linking of the idea of the New Jerusalem to Glastonbury through his presentation on sacred geometry in *City of Revelation*. Michell summarised that work and suggested that the canon of sacred geometry was in itself an archetype that periodically resurfaces, implying, although not stating directly in the article, that it could be placed alongside the things seen in the sky, and Atlantis, as part of the emotionally charged package active in the collective psyche now and particularly in places like Glastonbury.

The 1977 edition also featured an *Afterword* by Colin Wilson in which he briefly surveyed the Earth Mysteries scene of the time; Watkins and his leys, dowsing and pendulums, connections with ghosts, Stephen Jenkins Shambhala stories, and the wider spectrum of the paranormal. He would expound on these topics at far greater length in his immense *Mysteries* that would be published the following year. It is interesting that Wilson was unconvinced about the theme that formed the centre of gravity of the whole anthology. Having referred to theories about how the local community might have used the various sites in the Avebury/Silbury Hill landscape, he confessed that *'I find it very hard to imagine how Glastonbury's Temple of the Stars could have been used in any practical way'*. We shall come to see how at least a few individuals and small groups would interact with it.

Anthony Roberts praised Glastonbury as '*a planetary beacon and powerhouse of the spirit*', prophesying that, '*The revolutionary revival of Albion's true spirit will be the precursor of a New Age and that apocalyptic revival will spring from the eternally universal fountain head that is Glastonbury. The Day draws nearer*'.

EGYPT AND IMMORTALITY

WORKING WITH A profound belief in the possibility of physical immortality and that a planetary throat chakra is focused in Cairo, Robert Coon's mission involved ensuring that, *'the archetypal thought of Physical Immortality, the Key Word of the Aquarian Aeon, was energized within the collective consciousness of humanity.'* Timing was of vital importance in this grand plan and two major magickal acts would be involved.

Coon believed that it was vital for him to be in Cairo at the time of the 1979 Autumn Equinox. This was partly inspired by studying strange prophecies derived from the dimensions of the Great Pyramid, in particular by Adam Rutherford, who although meticulous in his adherence to genuine measurements, could readily be described as a Bible nut and fellow traveller of the likes of Jehovah's Witness founder Charles Taze Russell, who had earlier used the pyramid to support an extreme evangelical prophesying. Basically, the epoch of the Second Coming of Christ would begin in 1979 ushering in a millennium lasting until 2979. The material had very specific locations within the pyramid linked to it. The entrance to the Queen's Chamber marked the 1979 moment.

Robert Coon set out to be there at the exact moment of the prophecy. He felt that a new era was set to unfold and it would involve a shift in consciousness which he linked with his major concern, Immortalism. Following on from the prophetic moment in the pyramid, he would then immediately set out to rediscover and *'realign'* the Stele of Revealing, an Egyptian funerary item of great significance in the magickal system of Aleister Crowley located in Cairo Museum, and recite an appropriate invocation in its vicinity. This was accomplished on September 24th. A deliberate magickal link between Egypt and Glastonbury, the throat and heart chakras, was then made when Robert came to Chalice Hill a few weeks later on October 7th 1979. This was all part of the bigger picture of preparation for the Global Omega Point in 1984.

DARK GODS

THE GLASTONBURY ANTHOLOGY represented a peak moment in Anthony Robert's work. His writings were filled with light, infused with Blakean vision and passion. There can be no doubt though that paranoia was a constant companion to the great journey of the sixties. The decade seemed to be bookended by ritual murders involving President Kennedy and Charles Manson.

The success of the *Close Encounters* movie seemed to mark a high point of interest in UFOs and a positive interpretation of the phenomenon. There was one man who was not at all pleased with the film though and the story of this Glastonbury resident marks a change of mood that would engulf Anthony Roberts.

Eric Inglesby had watched the advent of the UFO era in 1947 with horror. A decade earlier, a friend of his, whilst in the throes of serious illness, underwent some spectacularly strange experiences involving visions of a coming atomic war that would extend into outer space with the science inspired by demonic forces whilst *'a battle was raging for possession of my soul'*. This suggested to Inglesby that the realm of space was one inhabited by the powers and principalities spoken of in the Bible.

By the fifties, he had firmly decided that flying saucers were demonic rather than extra-terrestrial in origin and began writing a piece on that theme. Leslie and Adamski's book constantly referred to ancient mystery cults, Theosophy and so on, a spectrum of subjects not exactly in tune with the church. It ranked as *'undoubtedly one of the deadliest publications ever to have come off a printing press'*. Fatima was a UFO manifestation and *'a master stroke of the devil in his plan of subversion'*. Inspired by some, though by no means all, of the work of Rudolf Steiner, he detected a Luciferic influence in UFOlogy that linked it with Nazism. This was a vivid topic for Inglesby, having been present at the opening ceremony of the Berlin Olympics as part of a British naval delegation. He had been seated very close to Hitler and been stunned and frightened by the messianic welcome the Führer had received.

Ordained as a Church of England priest, Ingelsby entered into extensive correspondence with a number of notable people across the British establishment spectrum including C. S. Lewis, Lord Mountbatten (with whom he had worked during the war as Assistant Secretary), and RAF figures known to have an interest in the UFO mystery, Lord Dowding, and Sir Victor Goddard.

His attitude hardened still further in the later years of his life when he took up an obscure form of the Orthodox faith, becoming known as Father Paul. Coming to live in Glastonbury until his death at the age of 94 in 2010, he continued the propagation of his UFO beliefs until very near the end of his life.

Inglesby wrote to the Archbishop of Canterbury and Lord Mountbatten in an attempt to persuade them that the Queen and Prince Philip should not attend the Royal Premiere of *Close Encounters* due to the dangerous demonic nature of the subject matter. His book *UFOs and the Christian* was published in 1978.

During the mid-seventies a number of leading British UFOlogists were coming to a similar conclusion, including Gordon Creighton, editor of *The Flying Saucer Review*. Some completely abandoned the subject. Randall Jones Pugh was co-author with F. W. Holliday of *The Dyfed Enigma*, a tale featuring a wide weirdness spectrum connected with some alleged high density UFO activity. After experiences that scared him so much he was not even prepared to talk about them he burned his collection of UFO literature and slides believing that evil forces were behind the phenomenon.

It was against the backdrop of this dramatically different mood that Anthony Roberts produced his last major work, *The Dark Gods*, written in collaboration with Geoff Gilbertson and published in 1980 with a lengthy introduction by Colin Wilson. It is a profoundly pessimistic paranoid piece that forms a stark contrast to *Giants in the Earth* and the Glastonbury anthology of only a few years earlier.

The authors were in essential agreement with the innovative and still controversial UFOlogical work of John Keel as best presented in *UFOs: Operation Trojan Horse* and *The Mothman Prophecies*. Like Vallée, Keel believed that one shape-shifting phenomenon has been interacting with the human race for aeons. He extended the range of investigation. It can be discovered in faerie lore and in the study of ghosts, telepathy, automatic writing, trance mediumship, poltergeist manifestations, vampires, and psychic phenomenon in general, along with anomalous airships and mystery planes from before 1947. All of this threw new light on the modern UFO events. Alien entities seem strongly similar to traditional angels and demons.

Very much at odds with most mid-sixties UFOlogy, Keel did not necessarily believe the source of it was off-planet. He coined the term *Ultraterrestrial* to designate the intelligences involved. As he later stated in *The Mothman Prophecies*, '*When you review the ancient references you are obliged to conclude that the presence of these objects and beings is a normal condition for this planet.*' Some other forms of consciousness are present here with us, albeit on an extended spectrum the existence of which is normally unsuspected. The Ultraterrestrials '*operate outside the limits of our space-time continuum yet have the ability to cross over into our reality.*' They can manifest for brief periods in a bewildering variety of forms.

Keel's *"Paraphysical hypothesis"* suggested that UFOs and their inhabitants originate in the astral realms familiar to occultists, mystics and spiritualists. Their bizarre home worlds that awestruck contactees sometimes journey to are not dissimilar to the spheres of the Qabalah or the Lokas and hidden kingdoms of eastern lore that blink in and out of consensus reality and can only be noticed by the prepared. Keel came to believe that human consciousness was an important factor in how the phenomenon manifested. The history and folklore of an area created a psychogeographical matrix that interacted with its inhabitants. Predisposition towards paranormal experiences was another aspect of the alchemical blend. The phenomenon was interactive.

After the Point Pleasant bridge disaster in the Mothman story, John Keel's feelings about the Ultraterrestrials came to resemble the medieval church talking about the devil and all his works. '*The demonologists have been studying the same thing as the UFOlogists.*' '*The manifestations are the same, only the frame of reference is different.*'

In *The Dark Gods*, Roberts and Gilbertson presented a case that malevolent entities have been messing with our heads since the dawn of history. Horror and science fiction cult writer H. P. Lovecraft was their unwitting vehicle. Just about every single esoteric group in the western tradition reeks of diabolism and general contamination. Freemasonry is a hideous tentacled monstrosity aiming at Luciferic world domination. And so on. The modern vogue for paranoia about the Illuminati, lizard aliens and suchlike, is in some ways anticipated but the authors are far more well-read and interesting than most of the modern proponents of such theories.

The fundamentals of the conundrums presented by ideas that connect UFOlogy with the wider study of occultism and the paranormal have perhaps best been characterised by Robert Anton Wilson in the *Cosmic Trigger: Final Secret of the Illuminati*. '*In researching occult conspiracies, one eventually faces a crossroad of mythic proportions (called Chapel Perilous in the trade).*' '*Everything you fear is waiting with slavering jaws — but if you are armed with the wand of intuition, the cup of sympathy, the sword of reason and the pentacle of valor, you will find there (the legends say) the Medicine of Metals, the Elixir of Life, the Philosopher's Stone, True Wisdom and Perfect Happiness.*' '*You come out the other side either a stone paranoid or an agnostic; there is no third way. I came out an agnostic.*' There are '*those without the pentacle of valor who stand outside the door of Chapel Perilous, trembling and warning all who would enter that the chapel is really an Insect Horror Machine programmed by Death Demons and dripping fetidly with green goo.*'

The eighties were a strange and difficult decade for Anthony Roberts. In 1981, in keeping with his long-term views, he resigned from his job at *The Times* following its takeover by Rupert Murdoch. A few years later, Roberts created an unfortunate furore in Glastonbury through his response to Feminists working in the field of spirituality in the town. Perceiving an imbalance in some of their work and hostility towards men, he produced a series of *Anti-Feminist Papers.* This is not the place to fully examine that situation. I tend to feel that the manner in which a communication is delivered profoundly affects the way it will be received. A twenty-stone man with the personality style of Brian Blessed was always likely to encounter difficulties in opening a constructive dialogue in such a circumstance. He didn't do himself any favours and was soon actively despised by a number of people. The reputation of Anthony Roberts remains coloured by that episode in some circles to this day.

LORD OF THE FLAME

IN 1981 PERHAPS THE MOST far-out of all Glastonbury Zodiac space brother offerings was published. Elizabeth Van Buren was a wealthy descendent of a nineteenth century American President who immersed herself in a wide spectrum of mystical weirdness. She believed that the Great White Brotherhood headed by Sanat Kumara had vacated their Himalayan base and migrated via subterranean tunnels that extended beneath the entire Pacific Ocean to a new hidden sanctuary in the Andes. She would spend time later in the decade living in the vicinity of Rennes le Chateau, coming to believe that the Merovingian monarchs associated with its mysteries recently publicised in *The Holy Blood and the Holy Grail* were of extra-terrestrial descent.

Lord of the Flame made Brinsley le Poer Trench seem a sober academic in comparison. Early on in the proceedings, the reader discovers what they are in for. *'The Secret of the Great Pyramid and why it had been placed on the desert sands of Egypt by our brothers in Space was revealed to me while writing this book.'* Before long, the big questions are getting asked. *'Was Christ a Venusian?'* Well, look at *Revelation* 22:16 *'I am the root and the offspring of David, and the bright and Morning Star.'* What exactly is that supposed to mean?

The somewhat controversial main theme of *Lord of the Flame* is that, *'Lucifer is Christ's twin brother'*. A Himalayan Lama is quoted telling Andrew Tomas that Lucifer was a *'godlike giant'* ET who had come to help accelerate human evolution. When the next cycle began, he refused to step aside. We are now entering the Last Days and the Lord of the Flame is set to return. The mystery of divine twins was a theme that Trench also examined. A sibling relationship between Venus and Earth is postulated, bringing in Blavatsky and Velikovsky for support. Castor and Pollux are the two brightest stars in the constellation of Gemini. *'Do they represent the Heavenly and Earthly Twin? — Is there another race of god-like men who live in the stars, our brothers of the Cosmos, our twin brothers?'* A whole mix of imagery connected with the Gemini figure is brought in to the discussion.

A lot of obscure esoteric lore gets a going over, including the Hall of Records that supposedly lies beneath the Giza plateau, that favourite figure of sacred mathematics and geometry enthusiasts, Fibonacci, and the lion-headed Mithraic Lord of Time.

Van Buren created a triangle on a map of the Glastonbury Zodiac between the eyes on the Virgo and Sagittarius figures and the eye of a generally neglected Griffon. This supposedly delineates a zone coterminous with the Great Pyramid. Superimposing its inner dimensions over the triangle puts the King's Chamber in the vicinity of the village of Kingweston, which Van Buren specifically names on her diagram. The church *'must certainly have been built over an ancient temple'*. It is not a place which had attracted outlandish mystical speculation before. She also stated that the curling of the Leo lion tail is formed to point towards the Queen's Chamber. Van Buren may be the most eccentric of all the cast of characters assembled here but some of her strange Glastonbury ideas would soon resurface and lead to a tangible conclusion.

ELLIPTICAL NAVIGATIONS

ROBERT COON was spending more time in Glastonbury as his Omega Point approached. His first major published work on the Glastonbury Zodiac was the superbly titled *Elliptical Navigations through the Multitudinous Aethyrs of Avalon* in 1984. This was later updated to *Voyage to Avalon*. Anthony Roberts wrote an introduction in which he said that, *'The opacity, facilitated by the jewelled prose, is a necessary initiatory construct that is designed to trigger the psychic synapses ... and so enable the reader to soar into the glittering realms of "another reality."'* This prepares the reader for a unique journey into the Zodiac, which Coon considered to be '*a Great Synchronicity Machine weaving myths and legends from past, present, and future*'.

Mystical poems, surreal juxtapositions of apparently unconnected but magickally cohering information, and outlandish prophecies, are woven in and out of expositions of his thirteen-sphere "Enochian Cabala". A vital part of the alchemical Coon blend is his acceptance and advocacy of the work of Aleister Crowley. There's a powerful Thelemic flavour throughout. He is also a great lover of literature with an appreciation of John Cowper Powys. The mix has not been to everyone's taste but from the moment I first read *Elliptical Navigations* in 1989 I was vastly entertained and inspired.

During this same period Coon spent a tremendous amount of time visiting the Zodiac sites and researching them in local libraries and museums. Mary Caine made a few adjustments to the Maltwood images of the effigies. Coon continued this procedure. The most notable example is in Scorpio. Katharine Maltwood had confessed to considering her delineation of the figure as being the least satisfactory. Mary Caine made major changes to it that virtually amounted to a new version. Coon dumped them both in favour of an eagle. This sort of manoeuvre lends fuel to the critics who would say that if it's really there in the first place then you just can't validly do that kind of thing. Maltwood and Caine thought in terms of landscape engineering by real people. Coon tends to feel that natural forces are at work, albeit divine ones, and the emergence of the Zodiac is not a finished process. The figures are changing in the present day. People do interact with them and help them along but something more mysterious is involved.

Katharine Maltwood and Mary Caine didn't really offer up any suggestions about what one could actually *do* with the Zodiac. This was an issue for Colin Wilson as well. Robert Coon had already figured out his methodology by the early eighties but it would be best expressed a decade later. In a 1993 booklet, *The Glastonbury Zodiac,* he stated that '*Things can be done in this area that on the macrocosmic scale connect and work out into greater dimensions, so I have always worked with it from the view point of what can be done working with the Zodiac can be useful for planetary healing, for spiritual evolution on the earth.*' In many of his works he recommends visiting sites at times of new and full moons and when the sun enters the Zodiac signs. So, to be clear about what that means, if it was a full moon in Leo, try and be somewhere good in the Leo figure, ideally at the exact time, even if that might be in the middle of the night. At the exact moment when the sun enters a particular sign, be somewhere on it and maybe ding a Tibetan bowl and offer up prayers and invocations to appropriate deities and angels and so on. Perhaps a whole year could be spent completing the circuit. It seems inevitable that interesting processes would be triggered by such actions.

Whatever one's opinion on Immortalism, Coon does seem to have validly identified a number of its motifs in the Glastonbury mythos. We have Arthur himself, dead but not dead, waiting to return. There's the Aquarian phoenix, reborn from its ashes. Joseph of Arimathea is powerfully connected with resurrection and brought the alchemical cruets of that process with him. The New Jerusalem blueprint can be seen as an important precursor to the physical resurrection seemingly spoken of in *Revelation.*

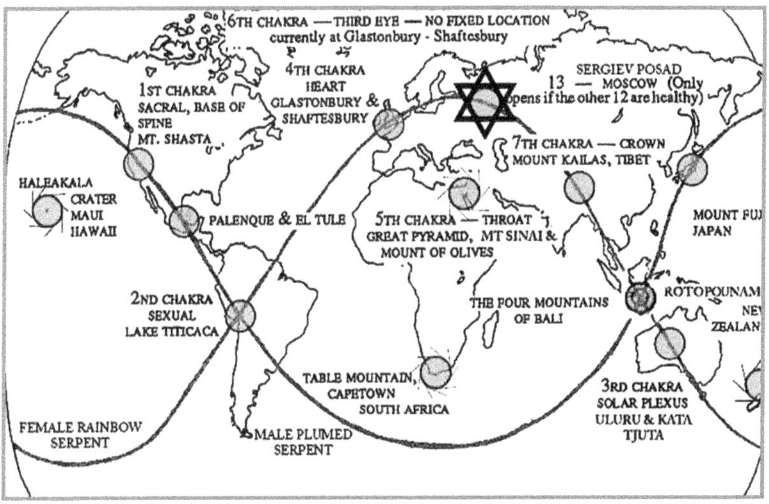

MAP OF PLANETARY CHAKRA SYSTEM

(© Robert Coon 1984–2006).

Robert Coon's Global Chakra and Omega Point theories are probably the most important new developments in Glastonbury Zodiac exposition. In yogic systems, a subtle internal anatomy is believed to be present in seven primary centres, known as chakras, located along the spinal column and up into the brain. They are normally symbolised as lotus flowers, of different colours, with varying numbers of petals, and a series of associations like the spheres of the Qabalah. Cultivating a harmonious flow of life-force through them, thus ensuring their proper opening and functioning, is an essential part of the inner yogic arts.

The concept of global chakras provides a context with which to understand Glastonbury's place in the larger picture of the world sacred sites and how they might relate to each other. Such locations are believed to be places of interface with the deeper levels of the mysterious planetary organism. Ley lines have been likened to the meridians of acupuncture, showing subtle channels for the circulation of the life-force around Gaia's body. The planetary chakras concept has now become a mainstay of New Age thinking although few credit Robert Coon with being one of its original advocates.

The first published reference I'm aware of that specifically refers to global chakras and their locations is in Thelemite Kenneth Grant's *The Magical Revival*, published in 1972. Coon is clear that he developed his ideas independently and his list of sites is different from Grant's although both share the same Glastonbury designation.

In Robert Coon's work, Mt Shasta is the base chakra. Lake Titicaca is the sexual centre, Uluru or Ayers Rock in Gondwana/Australia, the solar plexus, Glastonbury the heart, Great Pyramid the throat. The third eye is not fixed. He refers to a '*mobile Shambhalic focus*' which he believes to be currently active at Glastonbury. The crown chakra is Mount Kailas simply designated as Himalayan. Other New Age versions have put Shasta as the crown. It is, of course, not a concept responsive to archaeological investigation.

Robert Coon believed that the global Omega Point, which he conceived of as being small as a sub-atomic particle, was activated from Glastonbury Tor during a rare conjunction of Mercury with Easter Sunday sunrise in 1984. In the visionary realm, a crystalline green emerald rose opened within the hollow hill. He positioned himself to be part of the human side of the process. From that moment, '*The Spirit of that Summer of Love in 1967 has now been reborn in 1984 as the Phoenix rises from the Heart of Glastonbury.*' Fundamentally, '*the Messiah is the Global Omega Point activated at sunrise of Easter 1984 on Glastonbury Tor. We each partake of union with the Messiah to the degree that we dedicate our Hearts, Wills, and Actions to the unfoldment of the Great Truth of Everlasting Life now radiating eternally from the Heart of Ancient Avalon.*' A perfect expanding circle of clear sky seemed to appear directly above the

Tor and continue radiating outwards for days. This phenomenon was supposedly visible from satellite photographs.

Fundamental to all this work was the meta-concept of Aeon shift. With the start of each new astrological age, the focus of the energies of the time moves thirty degrees of longitude, or a twelfth of the circumference of the Earth, to the west. The age of Taurus was initiated around the Altai Mountains region. It was the beginning of what could be termed the Shambhalic initiative. The Zoroastrians presided over the start of the fire age of Aries from modern day Iran. At the start of each period there are deliberate connections made between the preceding and upcoming locations. The Piscean epoch was birthed in a longitudinal corridor that contains Jerusalem, Mt Sinai and the Great Pyramid. The Persian Magi are stated to have been present at the nativity of Christ. Joseph of Arimathea came to Glastonbury and not only brought the dispensation for the dawning Christian era but also staked out the location of the inception of the Aquarian Age. At this moment in time people will be going back and forth between Glastonbury, the Great Pyramid and Jerusalem. The next epoch of Capricorn will be anchored on the north-east tip of Brazil. The mobile Shambhalic focus shifts with the aeons across the globe and is currently conjunct with the Glastonbury heart chakra for the activation of the *"Aquarian Aeon of the Immortal Child"*.

LEY LINES AND LANDSCAPE ZODIACS IN QUESTION

AS WELL AS UFO PARANOIA, there was a further shift in the zeitgeist in the eighties that made the old Earth Mysteries blend unravel somewhat regardless of any Omega Point activation. The hugely successful *History* channel production *Ancient Aliens* has revitalised a corpus of work that seems to have come from a sixties and seventies timewarp. Erich von Daniken himself returned to confidently repeat what he had initially propounded forty years earlier with no concessions to any criticisms in-between. Once again the Great Pyramid, the Nazca lines, and the Easter Island figures were paraded as mysteries with an extra-terrestrial explanation. There has been no sign of the Glastonbury Zodiac though and there's a good reason for that. The other sites mentioned, the pyramid and so on, are unquestionably real. They are genuine artefacts of archaeology regardless of interpretation. The same cannot be said for the Somerset Star Temple. There came a point when a limit was reached on the credibility of the topic that meant it would be mentioned with decreasing regularity in works on ancient mysteries.

A good cut-off point can probably be found with the 1983 publication of *Ley Lines in Question* by Tom Williamson and Liz Bellamy, a critical attack primarily on the leys but also terrestrial zodiacs. The authors looked at the work of Alfred Watkins in great detail. He had believed that four sites in alignment was sufficient number to confirm deliberate intention. In fact it is not statistically significant. Unrelated features can be connected in groupings of up to four points by chance. Beyond that lies the issue of the kind of places Watkins put on his leys. They usually consisted of things from vastly different time periods. A case could be made for pre-reformation churches often being built on old pagan sites but it could not be taken as an invariable practice and the kind of evidence archaeologists like to see was often lacking. As for clumps of trees, ponds, marker stones etc, their apparent alignment could be pure chance. It was possible to create leys on maps using telephone kiosks and other modern features. The human brain simply projects patterns onto the environment. When it comes to the longer leys such as John Michell's Michael Line, the curvature of the Earth distorts map straightness. The line has to expand to be a hundred yards wide to accommodate this. Mention by Anthony Roberts in the Glastonbury anthology of a ley that links Glastonbury Abbey, Stonehenge, and Canterbury Cathedral was criticised on the basis that *'The three sites just do not align'*.

Having disposed of ley lines to their own satisfaction, they then set about terrestrial zodiacs with gusto. This part of the book was a romp. They scarcely had to bother refuting the subject. Even amongst Earth Mysteries enthusiasts the zodiacs were treated differently from the topic of leys. It was recognised as a far more obviously mystical and subjective study.

Firstly there was is currently no archaeological evidence for them at all. In terms of historical documentation there is also very little to go on. A great example concerns the passage in the pseudonymous Richard Deacon's 1968 biography of Elizabethan magus John Dee mentioning words written by him on an old map glimpsed in the Warburg Institute that refers to the Glastonbury Zodiac. This detail greatly enthused the advocates of the topic and is referred to in the 1977 anthology. A major problem arises through the complete lack of the fabled map for any subsequent viewing and the fact that the words quoted are in effect, as Yuri Leitch has recently realised, identical to a passage from Katharine Maltwood's writings save for an attempt to render them into ye olde English. What we are left with is an interesting clustering of suggestive place names but the antiquity of some of them is debatable.

The different features that mark out the effigies often date from a mix of historical timescales and include items of quite recent construction. The fact that the form of the figures is not necessarily agreed upon, and Mary Caine and Robert Coon made considerable changes to Maltwood's figures, doesn't help much. The main example at Glastonbury deviated in its design from the usual zodiac by having an Aquarian Phoenix rather than a water carrier. Cancer's crab is replaced by the Argo Navis boat but Williamson and Bellamy state that *'this sign is visible only near or south of the Equator, and has never been seen from British latitudes.'* Brinsley le Poer Trench's explanation for the missing twin to accompany the Gemini figure sitting in the boat, that it is in effect in outer space, probably wouldn't sway many sceptics either.

As for some of the other postulated zodiacs, one has only to contemplate the Aquarian squirrel of Pumpsaint to imagine how impressed Williamson and Bellamy were by them! The argument that the figures are artwork of mother earth and therefore alive and subject to change may be potent on a mystical level but is meaningless for an archaeologist or historian.

By way of a finale they quoted an amusing and ingenious critique of the subject by historian Richard Muir from his 1981 book *Riddles in the British Landscape*. He had used the same mix of elements favoured by Glastonbury Zodiac enthusiasts, particularly Mary Caine, of place name etymological gymnastics mixed in with history and folklore, to create a 'Glastonbury Bear'. For *Ley Lines*, he provided a further and even more absurd example concerning the presence of a Winnie the Pooh mythos in the Somerset landscape, ultimately extending its scale, *'for the whole of Britain was fashioned by Neolithic giants, into the shape of the pagan goddess Kanga, while 'Ireland', the Roo, leaps from her pouch to symbolise fertility'.*

The links between leys and UFOs had already become a fringe topic within an already fringe zone. The Earth Mysteries moved forwards in a direction where some sort of dialogue with Archaeology was at least possible. The Dragon Project measured

Ultrasound at stone circles. The concept of energy currents along the leys was to some extent taken over by the New Agers although the occasional old school text like the 1988 *The Sun and the Serpent* by Paul Broadhurst and Hamish Miller on the subject of the Michael ley still surfaced and showed the vitality of certain ideas.

AEGYPT: THE STAR TEMPLE AND THE GIZA PLATEAU

THE SOMERSET STAR TEMPLE has inspired some remarkable inner journeys and processes. Admittedly far from consensus co-ordinates and resisting historical and archaeological investigation, it could at least be characterised as a potent psychogeographical zone. We can grant poets and mystics the indulgence of finding results satisfactory to them in its multitudinous aethyrs but are always aware of it tenuous nature. Has anyone ever been directly led to something tangible by it? Something to give us pause for thought regardless of the criticism in *Ley Lines in Question*? I believe the answer is yes and the particular result in question and the path leading to it is in fact mind-bendingly spectacular.

Historical mysteries author Andrew Collins has produced a large corpus of distinct work that has been controversial and often well received. *From the Ashes of Angels, Gods of Eden, Gateway to Atlantis, The Cygnus Mystery,* and *Beneath the Pyramids* represent just some of his output. It is the last named that concerns us here.

In *Beneath the Pyramids*, Andrew Collins recounted his rediscovery of a cave system, forgotten by modern archaeologists, underneath the Giza plateau. It was the culmination of a decades-long interest in the subject of the fabled Hall of Records, an interest fully engaged whilst in the middle of a unique journey around the Glastonbury Zodiac during the nineteen-eighties.

Collins was one of the originators of what he termed Psychic Questing. Historical mysteries, usually with a mystical magical component of some kind, were investigated through taking psychics out into the landscape and being open to all manner of intuitive processes. There was a conscious suspension of disbelief in order to work with information from trance states, dreams, omens, synchronicities, and so on. If historical research could show that some of the material was accurate, and none of the details necessarily inaccurate, then it was considered acceptable to take a gamble and work with it. The most controversial aspect of questing concerned the apparent retrieval of physical artefacts from concealed locations as detailed in Collins' cult classics works, *The Black Alchemist* and *The Seventh Sword.*

In early 1983 a number of clues from different psychics and a visionary experience of his own drew Andrew Collins' attention towards the area around Glastonbury and in particular a place named Kingweston, which he discovered was situated in the vicinity of the Leo effigy in the terrestrial zodiac. Engaging with the clues and visiting the location triggered what appeared to be a past life saga in which Collins had been a medieval knight on a kind of Grail Quest.

Collins was further led to Dundon Beacon and, after a six month gap, to the Virgo sign following more visions suggestive of the time of the war between Stephen and Matilda, the mother of Henry II. It was intriguing that the sequence matched the way the signs had been revealed to Maltwood. The route didn't make astrological or geographical sense but he was determined to allow the questing process to guide him.

This early stage of the journey would later feature in a section of a BBC TV documentary first screened in early 1986 on *The Strange Affair of the Glastonbury Legends* where Andy and his partner of the time, Cara Trimarco, were featured at Kingweston. Remember that our attention was first drawn to the place by the somewhat eccentric Elizabeth Van Buren in 1981 who connected it with the Great Pyramid. Collins had no knowledge of her work at that time.

Bernard G was a man who had experienced visionary dreams and psychic states of consciousness for most of his adult life. Egypt and the medieval period were recurring topics. An intense dream in January 1984 featured a monk figure who showed him a kaleidoscopic mix of his entire inner life to date and recommended contacting someone he already had become aware of and intuited could help him understand. This was Andrew Collins, who was known to Bernard from Earth Mysteries publications of the time.'A subject matter was also recommended by the monk. *'Fate awaits you both in the church of Danbury. You must meet, and soon.'*

The church of St. John the Baptist in the Essex town of Danbury is home to a tantalising mystery. There are carved oak effigies inside of three recumbent knights considered to date from a period between 1272-1320. No extant records of the time record their identities. An eighteenth century vicar suggested that they may have been members of the St. Clere family, who held lands in Danbury during the thirteenth century.

In 1779 a "pickled" knight was discovered beneath the north aisle near one of the effigies. Within an inscriptionless double-layered coffin lay a perfectly preserved body, half submerged in a thick aromatic liquid containing flowers and herbs. It appeared to have been treated with embalming fluid. This strange find is not entirely unique. A few other examples from the same general period exist. The process had more than a hint of the orient about it, in particular, Egypt. Crusaders could conceivably have come into contact with such practices.

Following the onset of correspondence with Andrew Collins, in March 1984 Bernard had another extraordinary dream that seemed to show a scene from medieval Danbury. It was a fantastically detailed funeral procession. The style of clothing worn by various knights present enabled it to be dated between 1200 and 1325, matching the church effigies. One chain mailed knight on horseback displayed a heraldic image that was sufficient to plausibly identify him as a known local character of the time. The church was seen without its tower which further helped the dating. Bernard's immediate feeling on waking was that he had seen the funeral of William de St. Clere III and that he was the pickled knight. Two blue surcoated knights seen in attendance would have been William's heirs, Robert de St. Clere and John FitzSimon. These gentlemen are candidates for two of the effigies.

It was Bernard's communication of this dream in a further letter to Andrew Collins that convinced him that a meeting was essential. On one level, the Essex mystery was a self-contained topic unto itself. It led to one of his earliest works, *The Knights of Danbury.*

A larger perspective was soon revealed. Collins often drove down to the Glastonbury environs during this period of time to visit Zodiac sites out of curiosity and general information gathering rather than through definite psychic clues. At the end of April 1984, he made a significant discovery. It was in the church of St. Michael and All Angels in Somerton in the sign of Leo. Within the chapel of the Holy Spirit is a glass cabinet on a wall displaying historical information. The St. Clere coat of arms was displayed. The information shown indicated that they owned land in the vicinity. From the Chancery Rolls of 1303 a quote mentioned, '*Robert de St. Clere to collect knights fees for marriage of King's eldest daughter.*' Further research connected the Somerset branch to the

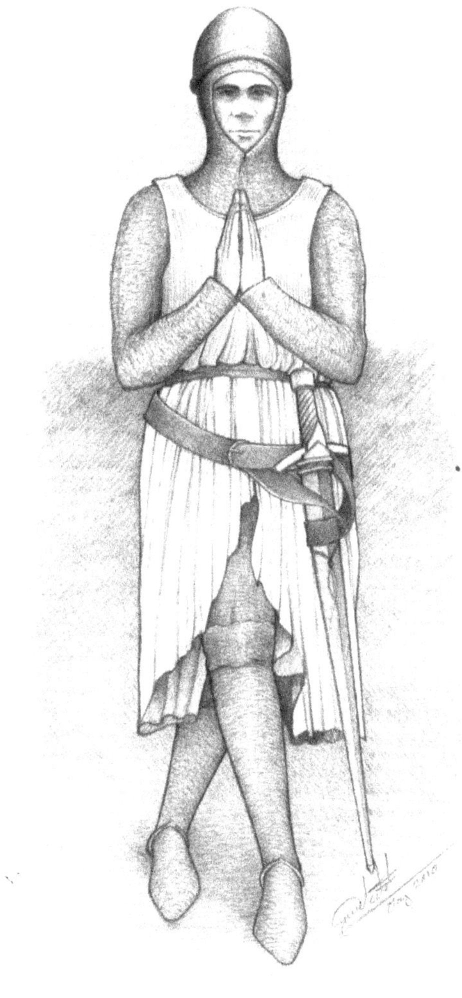

KNIGHT OF DANBURY, ROBERT DE ST. CLERE
(Drawing by Yuri Leitch.)

Essex group. The Robert de St. Clere who owned land in Somerton was very likely to be the Danbury man.

The coming months saw repeated visits to Danbury church and more dreams and psychic sessions that gradually revealed a compelling story anchored with accurate historical details. The St. Clere family were involved in a magical struggle with certain Templars. They protected the knowledge of an awesome ancient mystery.

In 1285 Robert de St. Clere was prepared by some associates to undertake a dangerous quest in Somerset. A mystical ceremony had been conducted in Danbury church. Robert was seen kneeling amongst a small group whilst another man made circular gestures and then cupped his hands above his head. Bernard saw these actions manifesting blue and yellow rays of energy that blended into green. A pouch was then placed around Robert's neck containing a ring with a six pointed star inscribed upon it.

Bernard was not seeing this from a detached perspective but through the eyes of one of the men present there. A name was psychically picked-up and later research confirmed the existence of the person in question, their life details, and a date of death that was in harmony with the visionary story. Phillip de Clara Vallis was a son of the brother of the wife of the king of France. He had travelled from his homeland to act as a kind of bodyguard to Robert on his journey.

During this same period, during the summer of *1984*, Bernard visited Canterbury Cathedral with his family and viewed what is known as the Opus Alexandrinum mosaic. He mentioned to his wife that there was a similar one on the floor in Glastonbury Abbey and it included a zodiac and lines set into the stones. Having virtually no knowledge of the Abbey's history he didn't realise until he spoke to Andy that it no longer existed. He was able to still see it with his inner eye so clearly that he could draw it and discuss it in detail.

The design on the floor of the Old Church referred to by William of Malmesbury and Bligh Bond's monks was apparently reproduced in the new Mary Chapel, signifying the position of the original building. John Michell had paid particular attention to it when suggesting that the Abbey's foundational geometry embodied the ancient wisdom code and represented the New Jerusalem celestial archetype during the Christian cycle.

Bernard saw an outer and inner circle. Within the two were twelve spheres, in four groups of three, containing symbols for the signs of the zodiac. In the middle of the inner circle was a square. Its corners could not be seen as they were cut across by a Maltese cross whose points reached out to the edge of the inner circle. From the sides of the square that were visible, four triangles reached out to the edge of the inner circle, indicating the cardinal points. Sixteen lines ran out from the centre of the design, through the twelve spheres and four triangles beyond its outer circle to sixteen small pillars along the base of the chapel walls, each about two feet tall, on which were further symbols. The twelve lines passing through the zodiacal signs could be continued out beyond the building to the locations of the fabled twelve huts and further across the Glastonbury landscape and beyond.

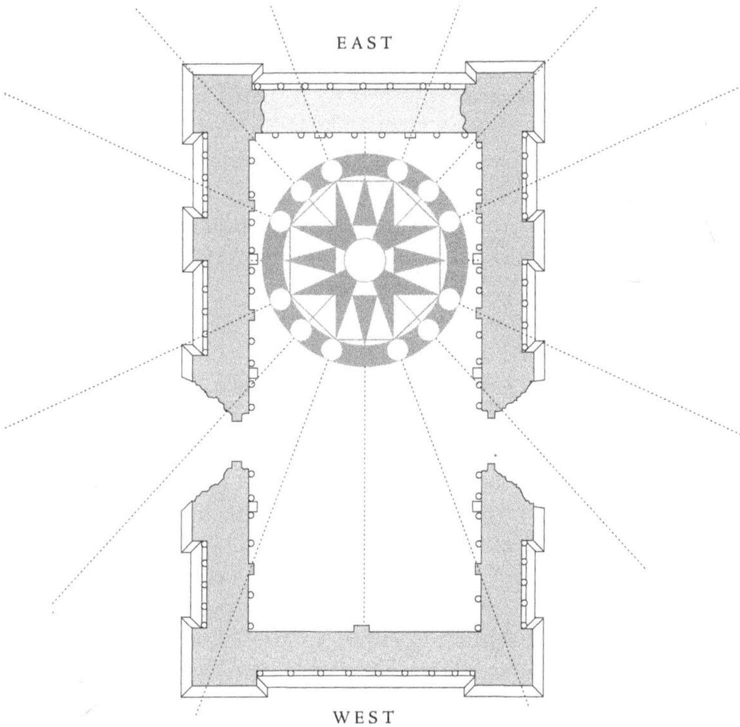

ST. MARY'S CHAPEL GEOMETRY.
(Drawing by Bernard Chandler from the original by Bernard G.)

The twelve zodiacal spheres and central point were coloured gold by ochre tiles. The outer circle in which the spheres were set was red terracotta as was the Maltese cross and cardinal point triangles. Beaten lead lines marked the geometry of the design. Somehow the whole thing was to be perceived as in motion. Each part of the levels of geometrical design was revolving. The Maltese cross was moving at one speed, the triangles from the square at another. A series of colours was produced by this that came to form one colour. The colours also had sound correlations.

Robert de St. Clere and Phillip de Clara Vallis had travelled together to Somerset in September 1285 and this prompted their apparent modern reincarnations to visit Glastonbury for the first time together at the same time of year in 1984, almost 700 years later.

In 1285 the mystic knights had been ambushed by armed opponents. Phillip de Clara Vallis was actually killed. The 1984 questers identified the location and visited it. The next day Bernard awoke with two strange scar-like marks on his chest and back corresponding to the areas pierced by a sword in the vision of his past-life death.

Robert de St. Clere had fled with the group in pursuit and was helped to further escape by some locals. A few days later he was ambushed again. Three mounted knights barred his path. One grabbed the reins of St. Clere's horse in an attempt to force him to dismount. He broke free of his pursuers.

What followed leads the story into more controversial realms which resist historical verification. Robert de St. Clere was led to safety at Glastonbury Abbey where he met the Abbot of the time, John of Taunton. He was led down into an underground chamber that contained a megalithic type stone, slightly taller than an average man. Robert knelt by the stone, with one hand upon its side. Around a horseshoe table were nine members of the St. Clere family in black monk-type robes. One of the nine put a kind of upturned cup on the top of the stone. He then ritualistically raised his hands and brought them together over the stone. As he parted them, colours could be seen in a similar manner to the Danbury preparatory blessing. The whole stone then became increasingly colourful. It started at the base with a reddish orange and moved through a rainbow sequence to the top whilst the man's hands were still over it. The vision progressed as the officiator then took a cup from the horseshoe table. It contained liquid. A few drops anointed the stone. This produced sounds, and the colours became translucent and moved rapidly up and down the stone until becoming pure white light.

Andrew Collins and Bernard G were led rapidly through the locations already covered in the quest, through Leo, and Gemini, into Virgo. At the prominent site in that sign of Wimble Toot, Bernard was led by a vision of a female figure to dig around the roots of a tree and recover a small crucifix. This was considered an auspicious sign. In Scorpio a further vision of a black knight on a horse barred the way and was eventually dealt with.

The powerful day concluded on Windmill Hill near Baltonsborough, in the sign of Sagittarius. Bernard saw a king sitting beneath a tree. This was followed by the bizarre sight of a huge bonfire with people walking in and out of it. Two rainbows arched over the fire that changed into a bird and flew into the air. It was holding in its talons a great multifaceted crystal. It flew over a huge green lake, dropping the crystal into the water. An island slowly emerged from the ripples. The bird was the Aquarian phoenix. It was the Tor that rose from the primal waters. It was a kind of Glastonbury foundation myth in the style of ancient Egypt.

Bernard began to suffer from high blood pressure and withdrew from physically following the quest although he pledged to continue psychically tuning in. It was believed that Andrew Collins should return to Somerset alone in 1985, supposedly the seven hundredth anniversary of Robert de St. Clere's quest, to complete the journey at the time of the summer solstice. The intervening period allowed some expansive material to emerge that deepened the perspective and opened the door to Egypt.

The zodiac quest had been split in two. At first it seemed that Bernard's apparently accidental high blood pressure was solely responsible. This impression soon changed. Only a few days after the autumn equinox intensive, Andy was back in Glastonbury. In *Gothic Image* he was idly flicking through a book on sacred geometry when a particular image seemed to switch something on in his head. It was a Fibonacci spiral.

Fibonacci was a medieval mathematician mainly known for his discovery of a sequence of numbers that seem to represent a glimpse into the laws of creation. The series begins with 0 and 1. After that, two numbers are added to get the next in an endless sequence where each number is the sum of the two numbers before it.

1, 2, 3, 5, 8, 13, 21, 34, 55, 89, 144, 233, 377, 610, 987,...

When a Fibonacci number in the sequence is divided by the number before it, numbers are obtained that are very close to one another. This number is fixed after the thirteenth number in the series and known as the Golden Ratio or Phi. For example:

233 / 144 = 1.618   377 / 233 = 1.618   610 / 377 = 1.618
987 / 610 = 1.618

Although not omnipresent, the Fibonacci numbers have been found as the governing principles of form in a spectacular number of examples across the whole spectrum of creation.

There is a particular kind of growth that develops outwards from its point of origin, increasing in size but not changing its shape. It is the form of the so-called gnomic logarithmic spiral that allows this constancy to manifest. Expressive of the Golden Ratio, it can be found throughout nature from the development of human foetuses to sea-shells. Fibonacci number ratios are also seen in such things as the arrangement of leaves on branches and the seeds of sunflowers to the breeding patterns of rabbits and the male/female ratio in honey bees.

These proportions have been considered to be the ultimate expression of aesthetic harmony, a glimpse of the mind of god at work. They have been incorporated into art and architecture. It has been suggested that the dimensions of the King's Chamber of the Great Pyramid are based upon the Golden Ratio. Once again, it is worth remembering that Van Buren had much to say about Fibonacci in *Lord of the Flame*.

This doodle taken directly from Bernard G's notebook.

In the following days, Andy started seeing patterns over the map of the Glastonbury Zodiac. Something was being communicated. Bernard was likewise being pulled into the matrix. He found himself staying up into the early hours drawing spirals over a map of Glastonbury. One over Leo. A larger one that took in most of the signs. There seemed to be a kind of inward and outward spiral that took in two sides of the whole circuit. Some of the signs seemed to be omitted. It wasn't quite clear yet. It looked like the course already completed could be encompassed within one side of it and what remained was the flip side. He also drew a gnomic spiral over his earlier design for the floor of the Mary Chapel.

Before long, the details were clearer. The path of the first spiral took in Leo, Gemini, Virgo, Scorpio, Sagittarius and Aquarius. It missed out Capricorn and Libra. The second spiral on the other side would feature Aquarius, Pisces, Aries, Taurus, and Cancer. There was a dualistic yin yang, light dark, alchemical interplay between the two spirals. The idea of a great wheel and the spirals seemed to be more fundamental than that of a zodiac, a word that the psychic sources were scarcely using anymore.

In early October 1984, barely a few weeks after returning from Glastonbury, Bernard had started to talk about a feeling he had that the sphinx is far older than the pyramids. He had been reading a remarkable book by John Anthony West called *Serpent in the Sky*. West mentioned that the erosion on the sphinx looked as if it had been caused by water rather than sand. It was still a little way off from the time when he would find a professional geologist to back up his claims and his work would become a major element of the nineties Alternative Egyptology movement. In '84, Bernard felt strongly that there was truth in West's ideas. He was also stimulated by all kinds of esoteric material in the book concerning the use of sacred geometry in Egyptian temples. His mind was being subtly primed.

A notable omission from the sites featured in the Robert de St. Clere saga had been Park Wood, considered to be the very centre of the zodiacal wheel. Before Collins' journey could recommence, the significance of the place asserted itself in a manner that ultimately placed it appropriately enough in the middle of the quest.

In February 1985, Andrew Collins learnt from Anthony Roberts that Park Wood was for sale. There was considerable concern that it might be bought by some dubious mystical group or unfriendly type who might restrict public access. It was clearly an important issue. When next contacting Bernard he was startled to learn that the psychic had been seeing visions of what he believed to be the very same place. In another glimpse of medieval history he saw a group of six people he understood to be Templars, wearing hoodless robes and moving slowly, first clockwise and then anti-clockwise in a circle, holding raised swords that were touching at their tips, to an accompanying low chant. The ceremony concerned the revitalisation of the land by drawing down the serpent's head and crown. It was led by someone named Americ de St. Maur. According to Katharine Maltwood the wood aligns to Draco, the dragon serpent, and its boundaries mark out the shape of a kind of Egyptian-style uraeus serpent crown.

Bernard entered into a period of contact with the knight. Americ later said that he was based in London and was the Master Templar of England in 1200. Research later confirmed that an Americ de St. Maur had been Master of the Temple from 1200 to 1216. He worked on behalf of King John and was present at the signing of the Magna Carta. This was a period almost a century earlier to Robert de St. Clere and round about the same period of time that *Perlesvaus* is usually considered to have been written. The ceremony was conducted at the time of the solstices and equinoxes. It needed to be performed again to ensure the future well-being of the site with the approaching sale.

Americ had also mentioned, almost in passing, a few other weighty topics. There was the little matter of a green tablet buried on the Tor. He had said that its

'Father is the sun, Mother the moon
Wind carried it, Earth is its matron'

There was talk of an arcane text *'from Espania, said to contain strange figures and numbers. Hearsay only. Comes from Holy Land. Very ancient.'* Toledo and Cordoba were mentioned, and the name Al Kindi. All of this served to focus attention on alchemy and Hermetica. The green tablet buried on the Tor called to mind the famous work, the "Emerald Tablet" of Hermes Trismegistus. When Andy looked more closely he found this passage within it.

'The sun is its father, the moon is its mother.
Wind has carried it in its belly, the Earth is its nurse.'

It was directly quoted by Katharine Maltwood in *Enchantments of Britain,* a work that Bernard had now read, but he had established an entirely different context. It is considered to be a core text of alchemy. Something seemed to be trying to link Glastonbury with Hermeticism. One story tells how the fabled green tablet lay in the hands of Hermes' mummy, in a hidden chamber somewhere in the Great Pyramid. An Egyptian Glastonbury Zodiac connection was starting to appear. The mysteries of Giza were now increasingly being pointed to. Whatever intelligence was guiding the psychic material, it wanted to suggest the strong likelihood that the mystical knights encountered in the zodiac quest had some knowledge of the Hermetic alchemical transmission.

Andy gathered a small group to perform a version of the ceremony in March 1985. Swords were placed in the ground to represent a crown. A pillar of light was then visualised reaching up from its centre, from which a revolving wheel slowly moved around the Glastonbury Zodiac at ground level, energising the sites. Eventually the wheel began to come to a halt and the energies were recalled back towards the pillar.

The Park Wood auction eventually occurred on the summer solstice, as Andy finally set out on the concluding part of the quest. It was a favourable outcome. Access remained and no dubious groups took control.

On April 9th 1985, Bernard was showing Andrew Collins his Mary Chapel design. He drifted into the Egyptian zone again, stating emphatically that there is a chamber beneath the Giza plateau. Andy was familiar with the famous American psychic Edgar Cayce's ideas. Perhaps primed by Theosophical and Rosicrucian input, he had talked of refugees from Atlantis travelling to Egypt and building the Sphinx and Pyramids. They also created a "Hall of Records", an underground chamber filled with the lost knowledge of pre-deluge humanity.

Bernard stated that there are twelve chambers beneath Giza. The great pyramid was built after obtaining knowledge about this. There was a link with the Glastonbury design.

Between April 28th and May 1st, he went through a brainstorm download in which he received a detailed design and explanation for the chambers in a similar manner to his Mary Chapel experience. Bernard came to believe that the underground complex dated from the astrological age of Leo, over 12,000 years ago. He didn't talk about Atlantis in the usual way. It was sufficient to think in terms of a previous cycle of an advanced civilisation that had all but disappeared through planetary upheavals. He referred to the "Elders". They were ethereal, extremely tall, viper-visaged, virtually albino types. They weren't standard issue Homo Sapien Sapien.

They weren't ETs either. It was a now extinct line but it had bred into the current human race. Their Crystal Chambers were not a repository for books and conventional treasure but a living cosmological temple. The knowledge it held was the understanding of how the present universe came into being. It represented the form of the process of creation and the actual point of creation itself. The rites that Bernard believed to have occurred therein had a haunting otherwordly feel to them that was both archaic and futuristic. They maintained, harmonised, and adjusted the very form of the laws of nature as they functioned within the planet.

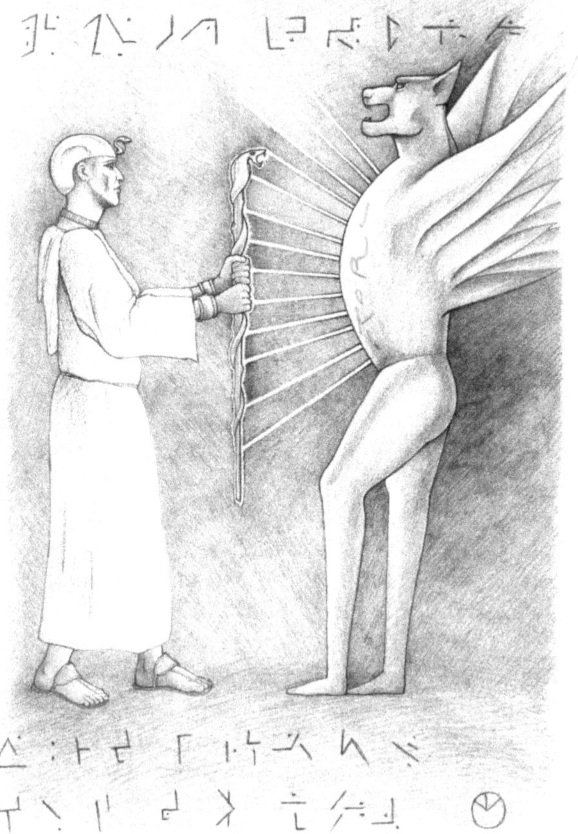

PRIEST AND COSMOCRATOR AT THE ENTRANCE TO THE GIZA CRYSTAL CHAMBERS.

(Drawing by Yuri Leitch from the original by Bernard G.)

The whole complex lay beneath a mound island on a lake. At the entrance was a large rectangular panel of polished grey stone. Depicted on this in base relief, on the left, was a man facing right wearing an Egyptian style headdress, a skullcap with uraeus serpent. He held a staff with a curved top. Facing him was a being like a lion and a griffin with upraised wings, standing up on its hind legs. Ray-like spikes emanated from its stomach. There was a line of glyphs between and beneath the two figures. The leonine being seemed to be a form of the Mithraic Aion Lord of Time that later became comparatively well-known in the Roman Empire during the Hermetic Gnostic era.

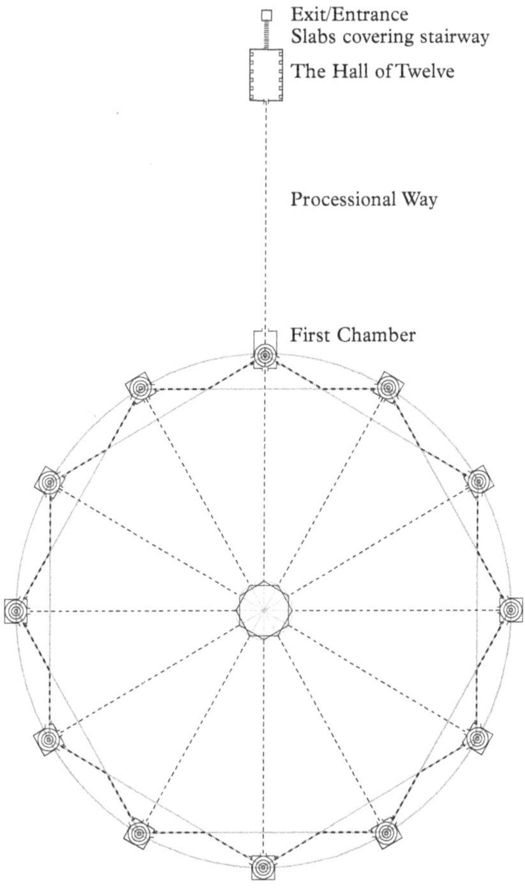

GIZA CRYSTAL CHAMBERS PLAN.

(Drawing by Bernard Chandler from the original by Bernard G.)

The ground-plan was in the form of a twelve-pointed double hexagram. Domed-roofed chambers were situated on the apex points. On the floor were a series of concentric rings, slightly differently configured in each room. From their central point of emanation, there were also three straight yellow grooves cut into the floor that formed paths outward. The left and right grooves connected through doorways with adjacent chambers, forming paths that marked the twenty four sides of the whole design. The third central groove reached down a long corridor to the central chamber producing a total effect like the spokes of a wheel.

The central chamber was twenty-four sided. In the middle was a twelve pointed, twenty-four faceted pyramidion crystal, several feet in height. It was the "Knowledge Stone". Its facets in combination represented all known colours, dimensions, aspects of reality etc. The last Glastonbury imagery Bernard had seen, at the climax of the first spiral of the zodiac quest, clearly recalled the Egyptian creation myth. Atum caused a hill of creation to arise out of the primordial ocean of darkness that preceded the first morning. The island became the sun temple of Heliopolis. At its centre was a black pyramidal stone with a quartz top representing the Ben-ben stone. The crystal reflected and refracted the rising sun's rays each morning. This was a living demonstration of a cosmology showing how the one became many. It seemed that the underground Giza complex with its central crystal was perhaps the original temple of this myth. The Heliopolitan form of it told of the phoenix bird that alighted upon the stone at the start of each new epoch. Bernard had seen Glastonbury Tor, the Zodiacal phoenix, arising out of the waters. It was an extraordinary mixture.

The Sphinx was a representation of the "One", the omnipotent guardian of all cosmic/dualistic dimensions. Far beneath it lay the central crystal, literally the place where form and formlessness meet. From there, all creation emerged. Time itself only began with the manifestation of form. It was considered to manifest in cycles of twelve, hence the twelve surrounding chambers. Each had an individual smaller crystal on the floor that would be held by a guardian who used it to in some way enter into the central crystal, serving as conduits for its unfolding of the process of creation. Bernard said that, *'To activate the crystal by the "laying on of hands" is to open the door. The mind leaves the physical, enters the crystal and experiences its facets of knowledge. The entire fabric of the crystal becomes as "one" colour and tone associated with the "soul" pattern of the initiate that swells throughout all chambers.'*

The complex had acoustical properties designed to embody part of a cosmology that used sound to express and interact with the laws of creation. Pythagoras is said to have taught that the Earth geometrically unfolds from a point in its centre and that sound created the universe. Three notes, D, G, and E, produce the keynote C. It is that combination that Bernard believed was used by the Elder Race in their rites of morphogenesis. The rings on the floor of the twelve chambers were two-dimensional representations of the cosmic tones.

Bernard felt that the apparent crystal technology was for real. The Elders really did plug into the matrix of creation and affect the whole planet. Things had gone wrong. There had been massive climate change and catastrophe. The crystals were globally dispersed. They're still about, albeit in some hyper-dimensional zone between the worlds. One had come to Britain. Glastonbury was always the main candidate for the location. The crystal's morphogenetic power has subtly influenced much of Glastonbury's subsequent history. Eventually, a diverse group of people will rediscover them and return to Egypt. The temple remains intact and dormant. It can be switched back on.

At the very least, it was a mythic fantasy of the highest order. Why would Bernard so thoroughly connect to such total strangeness? And why would it include so many echoes of themes featured in a seemingly crazy book that neither man had even heard of, *Lord of the Flame*? On the basis of his previous accuracy, Andrew Collins decided to take the gamble of tentatively accepting the scenario and seeing where it led. This was the beginning of the incredible journey that would lead to his later works *Gods of Eden* and *Beneath the Pyramids.* Most of the colossal corpus concerning the Crystal Chambers appeared between Andy's two adventures in the Glastonbury Zodiac spirals. This was, as always, significantly timed. It considerably affected the climax of his journey and what it ultimately led to.

Bernard had seen a dying sun king figure sitting beneath a tree, followed by the flight of the phoenix with the crystal over the primordial waters. Collins restarted the quest in June 1985 by taking up the imagery again. He identified himself with the king, visualising a fire springing up from the earth to engulf him. His soul was purified and released in the form of a bird. The soul bird then flew over the primeval waters of Glastonbury/Aquarius, a landscape void of form. He saw again the bird holding a crystal in its talons that was then dropped into the waters. The mound of creation emerged.

This visualisation was accompanied by a deliberately induced death-rebirth experience to physically recommence the quest. The setting was a weir named Baltonsborough Flights located on the forehead of the Sagittarian Arthur centaur figure. The Libran dove is positioned as if it has flown from Arthur's head. Something of this was reflected in the imagery of the soul spirit bird leaving the dying sun king.

The weather was particularly bad. 1985 saw the first of the great Glastonbury festival mud-baths. At midnight, the exact opposite time of the sun's maximum energy, in torrential rain, with the weir swollen with flood water, Collins jumped into it. On emerging, he felt the experience hadn't been dangerous or frightening enough so he jumped in again. Crazily, he deliberately expelled all air and sank to the bottom in order to fully immerse himself in the shadow of death, before going on to experience a moment of ecstatic rebirth. Not surprisingly, this process catalysed an altered state where his psychic perceptions were considerably enhanced. Subsequent lack of sleep further added to this until it eventually reached a hallucinogenic level of intensity as we shall see.

After a night of no sleep and further traversing of sites with visualisations, the Tor was ascended at dawn and the 1285 journey of Robert de St. Clere traced in the area of Taurus. The intention was to complete what he had apparently failed to do and board the Ship of Solomon, in the vicinity of Argo Navis, beyond Cancer, and journey on it to the land of the Grail. It was supposedly possible to hear the bell of the ship in advance of its arrival.

Robert had made a mistake concerning the bell. The obvious thing to do having first heard it would be to then head for the site of the bell itself, a place now occupied by Hurst's Farm near Dundon Beacon. Robert took a wrong turn and was ambushed again as a result. Although not physically harmed, his momentum was dissipated and the quest failed.

Andrew Collins heard the bell for the first time at the Hood monument in Taurus. He moved on to sit at the foot of Walton Hill in the pouring rain, looking out across the drove and rhynes that make up the figure of the Argo Navis Cancer ship, waiting for the sound again. He eventually heard it three times, coming from the direction of Kings Sedgemoor. With this came a vision of a great sea shrouded in mist. Above the distant horizon was a faint golden glow. From it slowly emerged an intense white light, the first indication that the ship was on its way. This was similar to Perceval's first glimpse of it in *Perlesvaus.*

The ship was made of wood, coloured red, white and green, taken from Eve's Tree of Knowledge. Its tall mast had a large sail depicting the upward pointing Druidic awen arrowhead. A carved griffon's head adorned the prow. The bow was tall and pointed, the galley wide and flat.

The boat eventually pulled up and docked. Andy felt beckoned towards it and jumped over a gate to enter a field where he could see it waiting. Again he paused to try and psychically connect to the scene more strongly. A gang-plank was lowered. He boarded the vessel. This was unknown territory. He had the *High History*, Katharine Maltwood, and Bernard to guide him up to a certain point. Beyond that he was on his own. A lot of the quest had already covered new ground. The climax was impossible to predict.

A number of sites were visited as the ship progressed towards its ultimate destination. Its appearance had begun a complete mutation of reality for Collins. He started to see it serenely sailing across the sea-like fields whilst he was driving along from site to site in his car. The journey climaxed in an orchard in Butleigh near the centre of the star temple.

Solomon's ship was steered by a gold and black-robed figure who was somehow Solomon and Merlin in one. Nine Grail maidens, blinking in and out of reality, sat around a copper cauldron of Annwn on the deck. A male and female lay on a plinth.

Out of the sea ahead, a gigantic waterspout appeared, more than a thousand feet tall, rapidly taking the form of a three-sided aquamarine coloured tetrahedron pyramid of ice-like light. As it was approached, it seemed as if it was made of crystal. The boat entered within it and as its barrier was crossed the vessel vanished although the feeling of being on it remained. All that was visible was a vertical pillar of light that was present with Collins, moving along with him though a void of darkness. Suddenly three shafts of horizontal pulsing orange lightning-like fire appeared, shooting towards a common source ahead. One passed right through Collins; the other two on his right. The source of the three bolts was initially seen as a faint red glow but the darkness began to recede as a sunrise became increasingly visible with the sense of the goal being Sarras, the land of the Grail.

Now the white light vessel came to be perceived as the soul bird, the dove of spirit, carrying Collins forward into the centre of the shining golden orange void of the land of the Grail. The three rays of orange lightning became white light rays flowing from behind the wings and tail of the bird, each emanating one of three divine tones. The bird seemed to somehow land, vanishing as it did so. Now, from its centre, the golden orange space could be seen as configured in the form of a large triangle. There were pillars of light at each corner. Red, emerald-green, white. Each pillar contained a Grail maiden who governed four signs of the zodiac. The one in the red pillar carried a copper chalice. Green had a silver one. White had gold. The pillars disappeared. The women floated towards the centre, drifting through golden orange light. They blended together as one white lady with a singular Grail. She was asked who it serves? The answer came back in a strong voice, "LIFE", as shimmering, she dissolved into a column of light. Powerful, pulsating, it moved forwards, engulfing me. All other imagery had gone. Below Collins' feet, a brief vision of a huge crystal rose opened a vortex that he fell spiralling down into, aware that the soul bird of earlier on had reappeared above and was rapidly descending with him. As he landed, it passed right down through him. Suddenly he was in a vast crystal lattice with thousands of triangular shaped facets. Looking at them, he saw himself reflected in each. The visions then changed into multitudinous glimpses of the past of the Zodiac and potential futures. The crystal visions faded with the feeling of being thrust into a great void of interstellar darkness. He could hear a low tonal humming drone, soon joined by two other notes, medium and higher. Blobs of light began to appear around him. Everything stopped. There was a deep red humming light directly in front of him, which he entered into and joined with. Back to primal creation. The point where all minds are one, where all is one in this and all other universes and dimensions.

Collins spent the morning after the completion of the quest writing down in his diary his immediate thoughts that undoubtedly showed something of the morphogenesis flavour of the Egyptian Crystal Chambers material. '*The Grail is but a superficial image created in a modern age. The true Grail is a multi-dimensional crystalline complex that forms the blueprint to cosmic order and form, from the centre of the universe, the moment of the big bang. It includes all life in this universe, its influence setting the standards of life for a cycle of time. It is the co-ordinator of the cosmic pulse of life and exists on many levels, the heartbeat of the world, it's a cosmic computer, controller of the destinies of Time.*'

At crucial times in the unfolding of the time spiral, some of the worlds' sacred sites open to allow new influences to re-encode the planetary matrix for the new dispensation. The present epoch is such a time, hence the revealing of the Glastonbury Zodiac, the call of the Giza plateau. In 1985, Andy had written, *'These heart/brain/minds of the Earth are not natural. They are representative of the central creative source of the universe and were placed here by beings who attained the stage of light millions of years ago. Cultures are co-ordinated to perpetuate the influence of their particular spheres, continually updating the existing imagery and archetypes, thus ensuring the quest can still be taken. This also serves the secondary purpose of a symbolic representation in imagery, stories and traditions of the cycles of the seasons, the cosmos and man himself, thus providing a place of learning.'* The *'beings who attained the stage of light'* were named by Andy as *Morphians*. Over the coming decades he would periodically ponder over what they might be. The medieval layer of site memory at Glastonbury was the last major update, hence it's powerful lingering presence.

An interesting timing symmetry can serve to conclude this glimpse into an awesome saga and perhaps point the interested reader in the direction of *Beneath the Pyramids*. On April 9th 2009, twenty four years to the day since Bernard G first spoke of his belief that there are chambers beneath Giza, Andrew Collins was in Cairo, meeting the famous archaeologist Zahi Hawass to inform him of his cave discovery, thus initiating a considerable furore. When lecturing on the origins of his Egyptian work, Collins always acknowledged the incredible contribution of Bernard and the unorthodox context that lay behind it. The cave system does not obviously fit the mythic vision, but there is a strong sense that more is to come and it was, nonetheless, a unique discovery.

CONVERGENCE

AS FAR AS Robert Coon was concerned, the rainbow serpents mated at Wesak, the Scorpio full moon, in May 1987 in the Andes, primarily focused on Lake Titicaca. This was the last major preparatory process before the Harmonic Convergence. Jose Arguelles managed to generate massive publicity in advance, breaking out into the wider media and being featured in newspapers and on TV. A template was set that numerous New Age events would follow in the decades to come. People were invited to visit sacred sites around the world during a three-day period but particularly at sunrise on the first. Robert Coon was strongly involved, following his own inner dynamic that had been established twenty years before. He served as the focus for some large groups of people in Glastonbury, on the Tor, and in the Abbey, at different times of the day. In his estimation, '*At Sunrise of 17th August, 1987, the Living Quetzalcoatl arose from El Tule to activate a new 52 year Heaven cycle on earth.*' Coon has never endorsed the work of Arguelles. He emphasised the Aztec as opposed to Mayan calendar and made no mention of 2012 in his general prophetic blueprint. Working with his own Melchizedek Cycle he noted that Jupiter was in a stationary position in the last minute of the final degree of Aries, the culmination of the process he was attuned to, at the moment of the auspicious sunrise.

In *New Age and Armageddon* Monica Sjöö took Robert Coon to task for ignoring the feminine in his Glastonbury Harmonic Convergence work. In his defence it needs to be remembered that as part of the 1984 Tor Omega Point event, he believed that a great female dragon current that encircled the planet had been activated. Harmony of male-female polarity was implicit in his concept of the two dragons.

The *"Planetary Christ Body"* had returned at the Easter 1984 Omega Point event and been in the womb until Harmonic Convergence. A further process lasting decades to bring it to birth was activated during the big year of 1987. This involved a huge grid of sites that constituted the "Planetary New Jerusalem". Six additional sites to the fixed continental chakras constitute the *"12 Planetary Gates of the New Jerusalem"*. They are located on Bali, Palenque, Mount Fuji, Haleakala Crater Hawaii, Lake Taupo-Tongariro in New Zealand, and Table Mountain near Capetown South Africa. Of these 12, 8 are "Driver Wheels", 4 are "Spinner Wheels"; the Great Pyramid, Table Mountain, Lake Taupo and Haleakala. A 13th gate was set to open in Russia during the nineties. Further unfolding of this data ultimately leads to a total of 156 sites finally fully activated as a complete New Jerusalem global grid by 2065. The grid is the body of Christ. The process of its creation shows the expansion of the Omega Point into an Omega Sphere. '*These 12 sites were anointed by the liberated Spirit of Quetzalcoatl.*' These details were published in a 1990 booklet, *Glastonbury and the Planetary New Jerusalem.*

With Robert Coon's work we seem to have come a long way from Katharine Maltwood. We must remember though, that Maltwood was thoroughly imbued with Theosophical Ideas of Secret Chiefs and Mystery Schools, and that the Somerset Star Temple was a product of their work. She would also have probably appreciated the idea that its emergence into our modern consciousness might be astrologically determined and very much part of a greater global mystical work.

GLIMPSES OF ETERNITY

DESPITE THE INCREDIBLE ideas and adventures so far recounted, the Glastonbury Zodiac gradually became a topic for just a modest contingent of New Agers, Earth Mysteries die-hards, and mystics. Mary Caine still appeared regularly at Mind Body Spirit events and her big green book sold slowly but steadily.

I consider it to be most heartening that, after the weird paranoia of *The Dark Gods* and the futile feminist controversy, at the end of the decade, Anthony Roberts returned to the subject of the Glastonbury Zodiac as if some higher aspect of his identity was communicating the need to somehow complete his work. He considered that the short article *Glimpses of Eternity* was the best thing he had written on the subject. In it he *'postulated that the macrocosmic Grail is in fact the geomantically far-famed Glastonbury Zodiac'*. *'The Holy Grail is the Sacred Centre: the generative flux of the matrix of reality. It's what William Blake called "the Starry Pole." It is God's kaleidoscope of dreams spinning in Eternity, threading inside and outside Time. The Grail is the beckoning beacon of Spirit. It appears in time of need and crisis, holding up the dimensions of Paradise as an ideal vision of structured , creational harmony. It fertilises and fuels the soul. It is a glimpse into the immortal heart of God. All these functions are equally attributed to the Glastonbury Zodiac.'*

A few weeks after the essay was completed, in February 1990, Tony Roberts achieved a legendary transition, dying of a heart attack on the Tor in daylight during an eclipse of the full moon. He is buried in the town cemetery, not that far away from Dion Fortune, with a megalithic-style gravestone bearing the legend '*From Atlantis to Avalon and Beyond*'. John Michell said at his funeral that, *'His life was dedicated to the Vision of Albion, the Quest in Avalon, and the fulfilment of the paradisal prophecies of Glastonbury.'*

VISION QUEST

IT WAS MY great good fortune to meet Andrew Collins in 1988. I soon got to hear of his own extraordinary adventures in the Temple of the Stars, a journey that would eventually lead him to the Giza plateau. Those details would feature in *Avalonian Aeon*. That book also recounts my own life-changing initiation into the material in June 1990. Andy tried the experiment of guiding a group of people around the Glastonbury Zodiac using his eighties journey as the template. What he had done over a period of two-and-a-half years, we would attempt in a 36 hour intensive with hardly any sleep and including such craziness as jumping into a weir at midnight as he had done in 1985.

I approached it as a Vision Quest. This particular term has become best known from the Native American tradition and exemplifies something present in most pre-industrial cultures. A candidate for initiation would deliberately go off away from their home to some place set aside from the normal world, some sacred landscape where the spirits of the ancestors were said to dwell, or the deities of the tribe could be communicated with. Out there, they would undergo assorted austerities, fasting, sleep deprivation, physical hardship. They would enter into a state where every action ritualistically served to reinforce their aim. That aim was a vision of some kind. It might be communication with ancestors or tribal guardians. For the hardcore shaman it could involve serious dismemberment, entry into the otherworld and so on. The vision would ideally become the central abiding truth of their lives, transforming and empowering them. I felt that, on one level, we would be entering a dreamtime with the ancestors, deities, and animal totems of the zodiac creatures. There would certainly be austerities of sleep deprivation and the ordeal of jumping into the weir to overcome.

The climax of the quest came at dawn in a wood near Butleigh at the centre of the Temple of the Stars. I made a point of writing down my experience later the same morning, the moment I woke up after a few hours of sleep. I'm eternally grateful that I did. Even delaying until later in the day might have diminished the emotional tone that was such a vital aspect of it.

The group entered into the final sequence of the voyage on the Ship of Solomon, using the imagery from Andy's 1985 experience. We went through the thousand-feet-tall tetrahedron pyramid of ice-like light, travelling in a column of light into the void of darkness. We approached the growing glow of the land of the Grail, now flying with the soul bird, hearing the three divine tones, and down into the triangle meeting the Grail Maidens and on into the crystal lattice presenting its glimpses of multiple realities past, present, and future, and finally into the great void of interstellar darkness with its three tonal humming drones. The blobs of light began to appear and then the deep red humming light directly in front of us which we entered into and joined with, being taken back to primal creation, the point where all minds are one, where all is one in this and all other universes and dimensions.

I saw a Glastonbury solstice dawn, symbolic dawn, dawn of the Aquarian age, New Aeon, New Age. Mists of Avalon are rising from the ground, vaporising into the air as they roll across the land. The Tor. The Abbey. Chalice Well. A hum, like organ music, gently but powerfully rising. A sense of the Abbey's perpetual choir. Celestial voices are emerging from the hum. On this new turn of the time spiral, other voices join the monks of the Celtic Church. There are native American and Indian intonations. Bells, at first sounding Christian, but then reverberating Tibetan style, sound a background. This dawn will bring a greater awakening and what we've done, our vision quest, purging and purifying ourselves, traversing the Zodiac in set sequence, we're in the same dawn, adding a tone to the great choir, an old tone that was known before, added again, but different in the way it relates to the greater whole, as this is a new era. What we've done, whatever individuals may or may not have got from it has contributed to the rising choir.

Glastonbury is waking. Now the Tor, a glass isle, a hollow hill, filled with elementals, ancestors, fairy folk. Vast angelic forms, Watchers of Avalon, are on guard. The Monks of the Company of Avalon are smiling, as the Abbey/Chalice Well current is absorbed into the beak of the Aquarian phoenix, the fire heart rising with the sun. In underground tunnels beneath the town, through the whole ground, the great humming sounds. All around, in enchanted sleep, are the dreamers, the mystics in Glastonbury itself. Because of all these people and us and what we've done, the choir sings louder and the inner bodies of those with right intentions are responding/resonating. Messages are being left deep inside. They are all singers of the song, though they carry different notes, different lines of the song. The more and the further they spread the notes and different lines of the song, the more people may start to hear the whole song. As they gather at places like Glastonbury the whole song will be heard more and more, louder and louder. We must resonate together and a part of our task is to revitalise the tuning forks of stone and wind chimes of water that are the energy matrix of Britain. A hundredth monkey point will come in this process: the more it happens the less anyone can do to stop it and at the quantum leap point- bang! - we're there, we're everywhere. It's all true. All that the visionaries have ever said of Glastonbury. It really is all true.

ADDENDUM: THE CONTACT CONUNDRUM

THE CONTACT CONUNDRUM concerns cases where subjects seem to be in communication with an external intelligence. It may actually be seen and take the form of a humanoid of some kind. It may consist of a brainstorm download, perhaps stimulated by an experience of light, where information and ideas not immediately recognised as part of the contents of the mind of the percipient intrude on consciousness and demand to be written down or somehow expressed. Investigation of certain subjects seems to help its manifestation. UFOs and Crop Circles are modern examples. The Holy Grail and the Pyramids are old chestnuts. And there can be mysteries connected with locations such as Glastonbury and Rennes Le Chateau that have the capacity to press initiatory on-buttons if approached in a particular way. Fifties UFOlogy is full of classic and often bizarre cases. We have considered the Adamski enigma. My *Aleister Crowley and the Aeon of Horus* examines a number of others.

The background to some remarkable ideas concerning Glastonbury clearly has recognisably similar elements. Robert Coon experienced a full-physical manifestation of an immortal light being who catalysed a download that took decades to unfold. He later had spheres of light containing immortals hover around him that oversaw the production of a great invocation. Anthony Roberts saw lights in the sky and suddenly accessed phenomenal creativity in which everything he had been studying for years cohered and poured out in a torrent of writing. The process formed the foundation of much of his life's work. The great psychic Bernard G, with whom Andrew Collins worked in the eighties, suddenly got switched on to the incredible mythos of the Crystal Chambers of the Elders beneath Giza. This had a sci-fi/fantasy flavour as much as *Giants in the Earth* in many ways. It did lead Collins to something tangible. What is going on here?

There is a preliminary explanation available that is fairly extraordinary compared to consensus reality but not too dangerous or fearful for our sanity to contemplate. A famous case from Glastonbury history helps our understanding here. It concerns the psychic archaeology of Frederick Bligh Bond at Glastonbury Abbey. In 1907 Bond knew he would be undertaking archaeological investigations in the Abbey grounds after the site had passed from private ownership into the possession of the Church of England. In the company of an associate with a talent for automatic writing, Bond asked '*Can you tell us anything about Glastonbury?*' The immediate response was the remarkable statement that '*All knowledge is eternal and is available to mental sympathy*'. After barely a few sentences further, they were fully engaged in the proceedings.

A huge corpus of material poured forth in the coming years. Some of it seemingly enabled Bond to locate the foundations of a lost chapel that no known documents gave details for. This remains contentious a century later. Other writing discussed the geometry of the Abbey and everyday life there. The sources of the communications appeared to be monks from the days before the Abbey had been destroyed. There seemed to be different personalities at work. Bond's understanding was quite sophisticated. He believed that in a place such as the Abbey, which had been the centre of devotion and study and a magnet for pilgrims for a thousand years, an atmosphere built up that became a reservoir of collective intelligence where much of the knowledge and history of the place was in some way stored. Human consciousness requires the activation of archetypes to access this kind of information. The figure of a monk from the Abbey's past serves such a purpose. It does not imply any spiritualistic model of reality. Bond was a superbly prepared mind, being an expert in medieval church architecture and a student of the paranormal with a taste for Theosophy.

This gives us another perspective on what may be happening with the Glastonbury Zodiac visionaries. They are prepared minds, fertile ground, and some frequency of the intense collective consciousness reservoir present at Glastonbury activates their reception to certain ideas. Archetypes of immortal beings of light and masters are simply the parts of the brain that need to work being switched on.

Aleister Crowley himself claimed to have encountered a discarnate intelligence named Aiwass that dictated *The Book of the Law* to him, allegedly a scripture for a whole new epoch in the life of the human race, so he had good reason to ponder what was involved. In *Book Four,* that became the introductory part of *Magick,* Crowley mentioned the mystery of how previously normal people undergo some extraordinary experience that permanently mutates them, allowing access to a power-charged state of consciousness through which they are able to affect great change in the world. The definitive example remains Saul on the road to Damascus who was suddenly overwhelmed by light and "converted" into St. Paul, the major figure in the creation of Christianity. Maybe he was epileptic. The debate continues. If he was, we could say that the seizure served as a vehicle for a transformational process that would have world-historical significance. One therefore hesitates to limit its source to nothing more than random internal physiology. Buddha, Christ, Moses, and Mohammed are also discussed by Crowley. His contention was that science would come to understand what occurred in such cases.

John Keel stated in *Trojan Horse* that an '*unknown extra-dimensional intelligence — controls important events by manipulating specific human beings through the phenomenon of mystical illumination*'. The most obvious spectacular modern accounts concern individuals who are caught in a beam of light from some aerial source. Making a similar point to Crowley on the St. Paul illumination issue, he noted that '*persons caught in these beams undergo remarkable changes of personality. Their IQ skyrockets, they change their jobs, divorce their wives, — suddenly rise above their mediocre lives and become outstanding.*' The John Travolta movie *Phenomenon* gives a bitter-sweet depiction of the theme that has increasingly entered into popular culture through the vehicle of UFO mythology.

It's there in recent mystical history as well. There are numerous examples. A few will suffice. In 1925, an Indonesian who came to be known as Pak Subuh was out walking late one night when a brilliant light suddenly appeared above him and then seemed to fall down into his body. Believing himself to be experiencing a heart attack of some kind he was able to get home and lie down.

Thinking he was about to die, he let go of all resistance.

Some strange force became active within him though. It delivered inner teachings and manifested an ongoing spiritual energy process that eventually was able to be transmitted to other people who in turn were able to pass it on. Such was the beginning of the movement known as Subud which continues to this day.

The mythology of Reiki speaks of its founder Mikao Usui engaging in a mystical mountain-top retreat that culminated in his absorption in a sphere of light which downloaded an entire system of healing and transformation into him like a lost Tibetan Mind Terma treasure. This was able to be transmitted by him and has since spread widely around the world.

Are there conscious non-human intelligences, entities of some kind, behind all of this or more impersonal processes? If you want to get occultists to foam at the mouth and start shouting at each other then bring up the issue of the Secret Chiefs. Perhaps the classic account of meetings with these beings of indeterminate physical status comes from Golden Dawn supremo Samuel Liddell Macgregor Mathers. Some of these encounters were psychic. He worked with his clairvoyant wife Moina in a similar manner to Mr and Mrs Crowley in 1904 to obtain much of the higher level Golden Dawn material. Other meetings were allegedly physical. He believed that '*they are human beings living on this Earth, but possessed of terrible and super- human powers.*' A terrific energy emanated from them that only an advanced adept could handle for more than a few minutes. It was strong enough to kill. Various intense physiological symptoms were reported during different encounters such as problems with breathing, '*cold sweats and bleeding from the nose, mouth and ears.*' Of course there is much debate as to whether Mathers created a fiction to enhance his authority in the magical group he led. Some are still willing to believe there may be some truth in his account.

Crowley himself was in no doubt of the reality and power of these forces, whatever they may actually be. In the late collection of letters *Magick Without Tears* he says of them, '*They can induce a girl to embroider a tapestry, or initiate a political movement to culminate in a world-war; all in pursuit of some plan wholly beyond the purview or the comprehension of the deepest and subtlest thinkers...But are They men, in the usual sense of the word? They may be incarnate or discarnate: it is a matter of Their convenience...*' This may strike those of differing temperaments as an inspirational or terrifying idea.

Even if Crowley's Aiwass was a true Secret Chief was he telling the truth? Anthony Roberts and Geoff Gilbertson were more than a little dubious about where some of the inspirations of modern mystics, magicians and UFOlogists were coming from. Are some occultists manipulated to further an agenda that was not an inevitable cosmic law of nature but a plan for mega demons to feast on the death of millions? They may not have realised. Indeed their conscious personalities might have believed they were working for an entirely different outcome.

Andrew Collins was initially a UFO researcher in the mid-seventies. His first sighting of an anomalous light actually occurred in 1976 during the end of the Sky Watch era at Warminster so he has tended to feel that, regardless of much hoaxing and delusion, a real mystery was present there. He has periodically renewed his interest in the subject in general. This helped his remarkable crop circle work in the nineties. In 2012 *LightQuest* looked at the some of the themes covered here, showing their strength through their ability to be continually revitalised with new paradigms.

It's not a new suggestion that UFOs may sometimes actually be living beings of some kind. The strict adherents of nuts and bolts theories of space-craft from other planets have been known to get uncomfortable with this idea. This brings together the lights seen in the sky and those that hover around the earth. It would explain why modest interaction with them is possible. The sixties Warminster Sky Watchers believed they could communicate with lights through torch signalling.

The lights emerge into our reality from what is effectively another dimension. When human consciousness finds itself caught up in the effects it may have experiences ranging from archetypal fairy lore to alien abduction, often in the context of missing time.

Collins takes the reader on a journey including plasma and 'bubble universes' that are interactive with human consciousness and catalyse a visionary virtual reality. None of this is actually purely reductionist. It doesn't say the phenomenon doesn't exist or that no exotic external intelligence is involved, it simply informs us of a number of exciting possibilities at the cutting edge of science that help understanding of at least some of the mechanics.

Collins crop circle theories and experiments had been inspired by the remarkable work of Trevor James Constable, author of *The Cosmic Pulse of Life*, and he returned to it again in *LightQuest* where he also discussed Meade Layne. I had featured the work of both men in *Aleister Crowley and the Aeon of Horus* and introduce them again for their relevance to the themes examined here.

Meade Layne was steeped in a wide spectrum of general occult knowledge derived from the likes of the Qabalah and Theosophy. In 1946 he was working with a psychic who was apparently in communication with a group of discarnate entities. Their teachings led Layne to believe that visitations from other worlds were imminent. This predisposed him to pay attention to things in a way others might not. In October a strange black torpedo-shaped object had been seen in the sky above San Diego where Layne was based. He considered there to be something sufficiently odd about the manifestation to ask Probert's inner plane teachers what it was all about. This marked the beginning of what may well be the first psychic investigation of the UFO mystery. The coining of the term Flying Saucer, closely followed by a nationwide obsession that would extend over the period of the Roswell incident still lay in the future.

Layne would eventually publish his theories in 1950 in *The Ether Ship Mystery and its Solution. 'The aeroforms are thought-constructs, mind constructs. As such, they are, in effect, the vehicle of the actual entity who creates them.' — 'The shapes and vehicles and the entity operating them form one being, just as a human being is a psychophysical mind-body unity.'*

Layne spoke of *Etheria* as the point of origin of the phenomenon. The term came from a late nineteenth century channelled text named *Oahspe* written by an American dentist named John Newbrough in a long series of trance states on a typewriter whilst overshadowed by angelic beings.

Layne's exposition of Etheria did not depict it as some other place in the sense of another planet in a distant galaxy. It is rather a location that is here and now when we have expanded our understanding of where we actually are and what its true dimensions reveal. Layne described humanity as walking on meshes of a huge net full of great spaces through which all manner of things can easily pass.

> *'The etheric worlds or Lokas are regarded as spacial and temporal regions of existence which interpenetrate with our world of (more rarefied) matter, and also, in their higher aspects, with the lower levels of the astral. Our physical plane includes the lower and higher etheric, but some four-fifths of this lies outside our normal range*

of sense perception. In this etheric region there flourish civilizations and cultures, and a race of beings which are born into that world and die there. They are NOT excarnate humans. They have knowledge of our world and can and do penetrate it. Many dwellers on the astral plane are aware of the etheric worlds also, and have the power of visiting them. This ability however, does not seem to be a common and natural endowment, but belongs to persons of a certain degree of development, corresponding to those whom we here call Adepts, or possessed of exceptional psychic powers of projection or clairvoyance. Anyone, in short, can function on any plane for which he is prepared, and astral vision and astral travelling is fairly common because of our interest in the after-death life; but the etheric regions have been little explored. Yet they are in many ways the most important of all, since they hold the key to ALL the phenomena of our earth life, and to the origin and history of our race.'

Inspired by the Root Races of Blavatsky and similar ideas of Rudolf Steiner, whereby the human race has gradually evolved from rarefied matter into greater density of manifestation, Layne delivered a radical perspective. *'We ourselves are etherians by ancestry and descent, for Etheria is the home of the human race.'*

Layne was predisposed to notice one of the more peculiar aspects of a number of early sightings. UFOs sometimes seemed to materialise and dematerialise instantaneously. This suggested to Layne a shifting of frequency between vibrational zones that exist essentially in the same space together.

The most famous mathematical equation of the twentieth century, Einstein's $E=MC^2$ helps us get an idea of how Layne conceived of the different levels of reality. Einstein showed how matter only appears solid on one level of perception. It could be said to be made up of particles that are moving so fast they are effectively solid. It's like an aeroplane propeller or the spokes of a bicycle wheel. Throw something against them when they are in motion and it will bounce off. In the process of acceleration and deceleration the blades and spokes are visible. When UFOs seem to blink in and out of visibility it may well be analogous. The vibrations involved are not the same as simple speed however. Although they remain on one level in the same bigger space they shift dimensions in order to appear and function here. They can be used for interplanetary travel but it doesn't mean they originate on potentially visible planets.

Trevor James Constable was a believer in the orgone energy that heretical psychologist Wilhelm Reich claimed to have discovered. During the fifties, in the USA, he learnt how to deliver trance messages from the Space Brothers. Some of the results particularly intrigued him. It was stated that UFOs in part are manifestations of previously unknown life-forms that live in the atmosphere. In the time between dawn and sunrise they can potentially be photographed using infra-red film.

Constable's remarkable journey was described in 1976's *The Cosmic Pulse of Life*, a work indubitably worthy of cult classic status. Perhaps the most important issue he raises is the role of the state of consciousness of consensus humanity in the UFO experience. As Meade Layne had realised, the changing vibrational frequency effects whereby UFO phenomenon became periodically visible imply that they are present most of the time but outside the range of normal perception. Cleansing the doors of perception does seem of fundamental importance and this doesn't simply mean consuming hallucinogens.

The inspirations Constable received from his initial trance channelings proved to be fruitful. In 1957 he went out into the Mojave with a colleague to try and photograph the generally invisible life forms in the sky that he came to refer to as "critters". It was considered to be a vital part of the procedure for Constable to perform a kind of meditational invocation to attract them. Facing east at dawn, Constable began with the assumption of an obvious star posture involving legs spread apart and arms held out parallel to the ground. He gently oscillated his body to try and atune with the Earth's magnetic fields. Having found to his satisfaction the resonance point in the east, he would then turn 180° around to the right to find it again. A further 90° turn to the right followed while facing north, then 180° to the south on the right. A 270° turn to the right to face the east and begin again completed the first sequence. Between sixty to one hundred repetitions would be performed around dawn. This produced what Constable called *'a regular pattern of bioenergetic pulsations in the ether.'* A beacon of this nature would be noticeable in supersensible realms.

Amazingly enough the duo photographed over a hundred biological looking images and more standard UFO-type "craft". The "bioforms" were pretty big, sometimes miles long. Constable believed them to have a kind of consciousness and intelligence. His record of this work and speculation on its meaning in the 1958

They Live in the Sky and *The Cosmic Pulse of Life* continues to inspire new generations. He believed the creatures arose out of the cosmic energy ocean of orgone described by Wilhelm Reich.

In 1962 in Ray Palmer's *Flying Saucers* magazine Kenneth Arnold, the man whose experience had started the whole UFO furore in 1947 and had investigated the mystery ever since, suggested that the saucers *'are not space ships from another planet at all, but are groups and masses of living organisms that are as much a part of our atmosphere and space as the life we find in the oceans. The only major difference in the space and atmospheric organisms is that they have the natural ability to change their densities at will.'* This obviously helped Constable to feel that he was on the right track.

Over the years it has been increasingly recognised that some of the lights in the sky reported as UFOs are manifestations of what have been termed Earth Lights. Studies have shown that assorted stresses and strains in the earth's crust generate electromagnetic responses that can result in the discharge of various types of lights

Perhaps the best example of the profound mysteries involved comes from a study conducted during the eighties at Hessdalen in Norway. The remote valley had become known for lights in the sky and a long term stake-out was arranged by various UFO groups. Many sightings and photographs resulted but the most notable thing was the way the lights gave the impression of somehow interacting with the observers. A modest example occurred when a slow moving light that was flashing with a regular rhythm changed its rate when a laser light was pointed at it. At the extreme end of the weirdometer a group of lights once gathered together to form a Christmas tree design and most absurdly of all, an unmistakeable depiction of the iconic billowing-skirt image of Marilyn Monroe. All of this can still be interpreted as linked with orgone.

To quote Andrew Collins in his development of Reich and Constable's work investigating the crop circle enigma, *The Circlemakers, 'Each time we come into contact with one of these dense orgone masses through close encounters, we give it identity. Its base intelligence is continually re-programmed until it takes on some semblance of the very entities we believe it to be' — 'The orgone bioforms are the alien intelligences and the fairy folk of old, and both are generated, programmed and updated by us.'*

So at least some of the UFO phenomenon may be a part of the still unknown life of the planet. This potentially links in with the Ultraterrestrial hypothesis of John Keel and the Magonia studies of

Jacques Vallee. We may have found the stuff of which these dreams are made and something of how they come to manifest. Human consciousness is central to the equation but the question still remains as to whether it is being acted on from outside and how far outside that might be? Orgone bioforms and Earth Lights may serve as a conduit for Ultraterrestrials and Inter-dimensionals. Anything that malleable could filter forces through into the life of humanity from outside the planet, from space. Clearly we have arrived in a zone crucial to the understanding of all forms of magic.

Constable did draw a distinction between the orgone critter sky creatures and the etheric vehicles of the UFO beings. He took on Meade Layne's *Ether Ship* terminology. There is a diagram in *Cosmic Pulse* of one of the interdimensional craft and one of his published Mojave photos is claimed to show just such a thing briefly making itself visible. Whilst being willing to accept that some of the things seen in the sky may have a nuts and bolts explanation as machines from other worlds he felt that the majority were not.

In *LightQuest* Andrew Collins outlined all of these general principles and went on to clearly state that the nature of what is seen and experienced is also determined by the location. The book is in many ways a guide to many places, primarily in the USA and Great Britain, where the best mix of strange phenomenon might be experienced, from folkloric entities to apparent aliens, timeslips and suchlike. There are all kinds of geomagnetic factors at play and much scientific investigation has already happened. Collins discusses some astonishing previously unpublished cases of extreme weirdness from crop circle country, the vicinity of Avebury and Silbury Hill. This is a development of the old UFO and leys theories. The lights and general weirdness do cluster around some sacred sites but not necessarily for the reasons that Tony Wedd might have given.

LightQuest bypasses Glastonbury but I tend to feel that it carries its own distinct version of this. We have noted a few modern tales of lights and the Tor. We have briefly met Gino Gennaro who encountered Fairy Venusians there and received a profound teaching from them. This uncanny hill seemingly has the ability to stimulate all manner of wild ideas about itself. An invisible castle of the King of the Fairies exists in the same space. A morphogenesis crystal from the Giza chamber is at work on the programme of the inscrutable morphians, emanating the star temple. A brain pattern is pulsating from around the Tor and helping to activate the World

Sensorium and all the more powerfully since the Global Omega Point was activated within it. It is the centre of a resurrecting bird of fire, returning for a new time cycle. That's quite a combination. And it seems to be interactive inasmuch as the shapes emanated around the landscape change form with passing time and the nature of the people who see them. Even if all of these ideas seem deluded or downright crazy, it still remains a remarkable thing that a hill and a landscape can inspire them.

Perhaps these experiences and light phenomenon originate in Reiser's psi field, '*the "world sensorium"- the guiding field which controls the psychosocial evolution of mankind'?* If Robert Coon and Oliver Reiser are to be believed then Glastonbury had been perfectly primed for the climax of Andrew Collins' adventure. Omega Point activated from field pattern for World Sensorium. Glastonbury to Giza Elder Crystal Chambers. Perhaps Maltwood, Roberts, Coon, and Collins are '*individual persons serving as the "neuroblasts" of the creature*', ie the great Earth being coming to consciousness of itself with some help from beyond, the morphogenetic field pattern formed by morphians? Maybe.

AFTERWORD

LOCAL ARTIST AND WRITER Yuri Leitch intuited a modern convergence of diverse talents united in their appreciation of the Glastonbury Zodiac theme and convened *The Maltwood Moot* as an occasional gathering that rapidly began to generate the new anthology *Signs and Secrets*. The subject has by no means been exhausted. Fresh genuine research into the life of Katharine Maltwood complements the more visionary effusions. A new mega alignment, the Melkarth Line, has been postulated, regardless of the arguments of Williamson and Bellamy. Does this just mean there is no time limit on credulity? What is our best response to this?

It would not seem outlandish to recommend to a lover of poetry a reading course in the early nineteenth century Romantics such as Wordsworth, Keats, Shelley, Byron, and the unique William Blake. These people had some knowledge of British prehistory, of religious studies in general, that would seem lacking or wrong-headed by modern standards. Their sensibilities were obviously shaped by their times, the French revolution and subsequent wars and so on. We don't have to believe in the reality of a Druid Stonehenge to appreciate Blake's art and poetry.

I feel that there is a kind of poetry in John Foster Forbes, Desmond Leslie, Brinsley le Poer Trench, certainly John Michell, and in the worldview demonstrated in Anthony Roberts' *Giants in the Earth*. I believe there is also something vitally important in the kind of mysterious experience that befell the Roberts near the Kingston by-pass and in the weird trickster life of a figure like Adamski. Some mercurial force was at work through all this, loosening the *'mind forg'd manacles'*, opening the *'doors of perception'* enough to awaken us from *'single vision'*.

In this we can appreciate one of Anthony Roberts' most potent ideas that I feel is his most significant contribution to the field of the Earth Mysteries: *Geomythics*. He wrote in the Foreword to the anthology of '*Myths that coalesce the physical aspect of specific place and object with the relatedly subtle forces of symbolic patterns and their functioning supernatural powers, as seen through the processes of magic*'. The Glastonbury Zodiac was '*a perfect geomythical symbol*'.

In *Avalon of the Heart* Dion Fortune wrote how *'the poetry of the soul writes itself at Glastonbury'*. I would say that soul poetry is present in the visionary works inspired by the Glastonbury Zodiac idea and that its fantastic realism is still at work in Glastonbury, as I can see by the people walking past my window on their way to the Holy Well and the Hill of Vision. It's present in *Signs and Secrets* and I hope it is present in these pages as well. We can comprehensively deconstruct the mythology of the place in terms of history but it's that elusive something else that matters. Beyond the changing moods of passing decades, we can still find inspiration here, now.

APPENDIX: ANUBIS AT BURROW MUMP: ISIS OF AVALON & COSMIC TRIGGER

FOLLOWING MY EXPERIENCES IN 1990 I found it easy to conceive of visualisations in the Glastonbury landscape using imagery inspired by the star temple. I include this example to show the kind of effects on the imagination that extended exposure to the Glastonbury Zodiac mythos can produce. The way in which it tended to spontaneously emerge was extremely satisfying and although in certain respects it could be considered to be a kind of artistic creation, the mood accompanying it suggests to me something more although I cannot expect all readers to accept that.

One particular time of year seemed to stimulate this process. Robert Anton Wilson's *Cosmic Trigger* is my most-read book. Its multiple topics cohere around the so-called Sirius Mystery, the title of a hugely influential 1976 ancient astronaut book by Robert Temple that suggested contact of some kind between humans and beings from the Sirius star system that left traces in Sumero-Babylonian and Egyptian religious mythology. Wilson expanded the context to ponder the possibilities of a continued secret tradition incorporating some ideas and motifs of this alien cultural package that has emerged in modern times in the work of the two great controversial modern magi, Aleister Crowley and George Gurdjieff. This is a topic I investigate in some depth in my *Aleister Crowley and the Aeon of Horus.*

Sufficient to say here that Wilson's research stimulated strange synchronistic events that could be interpreted as indicating he had tuned in to what could be termed the Sirius current. On one occasion, on July 22nd 1973, he performed a customised Crowleyan ceremony. The next morning he *'awoke with an urgent message from Dreamland'*. It stated that *'Sirius is very important.'* Looking for relevant information in his occult books, he struck gold in Kenneth Grant's *The Magical Revival.* Wilson was impressed to read that *'Phoenix was Crowley's secret name in the Ordo Templi Orientis ... The Phoenix was also an ancient constellation in which Sothis, or Sirius, was the chief star.' 'Crowley identified the heart of his magical current with one particular Star. In Occult Tradition, this is "the sun behind the sun," the Hidden God, the vast star Sirius.'* Indeed, the Order that Crowley created himself, the AA, has been generally taken to mean "Argenteum Astrum" or Silver Star. The part of Wilson that was a careful researcher hesitated to weird-out too much as he had looked through some of Grant's book before and may have subconsciously absorbed some of the data.

Later on, at a public library, his doubts were dissolved. He read that July 23rd, that very day, was the date when the so-called "dog days" began. Sirius has come to be known as the dog star. This dates from Graeco-Roman times. It's located in the constellation of Canis Major, the Great Dog. It follows Orion the hunter as the dog at his heels. The ancient Egyptian calendar began when it was seen to rise above the horizon, behind the sun, at dawn, after a long period of absence from the sky. This return was noted across the classical world as the beginning of the season of scorching summer sun, the dog days. In Egypt, it was once broadly synchronised with the inundation of the Nile. The river dominated the agricultural cycle of Egyptian life so it was inevitable that the star heralding the season of its blessings would be regarded as important. To the Egyptians, Sirius was the star of the Goddess Isis. The river's fertile gifts could easily be associated with a divine mother. Despite the preponderance of Egyptian motifs in Thelemic magick, Grant also traces its lineage to Sumero-Babylonian times.

Wilson was obviously stunned by this. He couldn't resist speculating as to whether, via Crowley's work, he may have tuned in to a magickal frequency that really did link Earth to Sirius through hyperspace. Somehow he had been led to the most auspicious date in the calendar to make that connection. From that moment on, for period of about a year, Wilson was willing to entertain the possibility that he might be in contact with some kind of intelligence connected with Sirius.

It is worth noting that the Sirius date may have been true once but it's not anymore. The date has shifted. It is now in early August. What I have come to respect is that the July 22/23 time remains a most potent magical time to connect with certain energies.

All of this stimulated my Glastonbury Zodiac imagination by connecting Sirius with the image of the phoenix, thereby evoking the Tor, and also later connecting Burrow Mump, the nose of the guardian dog figure with Anubis. This did not mean that I considered the effigies to be linked to Sirius in the star temple itself. In terms of the planisphere overlay of Maltwood, that Robert Coon elaborated upon in his own work, Sirius aligns with a well near Somerton in the vicinity of the Leo figure. Nonetheless, imagery readily came to me that was so vivid and made such good use of all kinds of material in my mental filing cabinet that I felt it was entirely acceptable to use what could be termed magical artistic licence providing no dogmatism arose from any results. The form of Isis of Avalon, inspired by the High Priestess card of the Tarot, is primarily that of the famous vision of the goddess from *The Golden Ass* of Apuleius. The details of her appearance and the mood invoked have been enhanced with details from various sources, primarily Dion Fortune and Aleister Crowley, that I was familiar with.

The visualisation presented here is an extended version of material featured in my *Avalonian Aeon* that formed part of the Tor-top climax of the narrative in 1992. The initial details using the four sons of Horus was the inspiration of Alex Langstone. A 1996 follow-up included the additional location of Burrow Mump and imagery of Anubis. It is all recounted in its complete 1996 version.

On July 23rd I gathered a car full of people for a visualisation meditation in the ruined church of St Michael on the 'mini-Tor' of Burrow Mump, considered to be the nose of the guardian of the Glastonbury Zodiac, the 'girt' dog. I intended to see it in the form of Anubis, in turn the guardian of Isis/Sirius.

My partner of the time, Chandira Hensey, had painted a picture of Anubis that was about four feet long. It was fixed to the wall of the ruined church. We orientated ourselves. The Tor can be seen from the Mump. A fix was taken on it. The general location of the Zodiac was briefly scanned. We then visualised a transparent blue sphere encompassing us. The building faded until only barely visible. An an enormous recumbent form then arose from the ground around us. Our sphere floated in front of his face. Flaming red eyes suddenly opened. Behind him, the outline forms of the Zodiac effigies lit up across the landscape. Above the Tor, a point of light was seen in the sky. A beam now came down from it into the Aquarian phoenix. The whole thing was very easy to visualise. The general consensus was that it was like watching something that was already happening rather than creating it through imagination.

We then drove to the Tor. On its summit, by the direction-finding plinth, we began by visualising the whole of the Tor hill as flat. At each corner of the tower stood one of the Watchers of Avalon, the indigenous site Guardians, seen as tall dark hooded figures.

For our purposes the guardians of the four quarters were to be the four sons of Horus. In the east was Duamutef. He had a jackal head like Anubis. In the west was the hawk-headed Quebsenuf. Ape-headed Hapi guarded the north. Imsety, with human head, false Egyptian beard and painted eyes took the south.

We started to walk slowly, anti-clockwise, around our circle, seeing the maze, the morphogenetic field pattern for the embryogenesis of the world sensorium, lighting up from beneath the ground in a gentle golden glow, activating the vortex to bring the energy down. Mists of Avalon were visualised as rising all around us until the whole world had disappeared, apart from the flattened shining maze and Tor tower.

The four sons of Horus hovered just above the edge of the glowing maze, against the background of mist. Thus prepared, the space was ready to receive the celestial energy. A small ball of light was seen in the sky, the body of Nuit, directly above us. The Isis/Sirius force came down in the form of a golden beam. Like lightning kundalini it downloaded into the Grail receptacle maze brain of the phoenix, sending ripples of light out through the spiral pattern.

As it did so, a majestic form became visible in the sky beside the Tor. A silvery cloud of pale moon mist formed a shimmering pillar that spanned the space from sky to earth. Beneath the heaven tree of stars hung with humid night blue fruit, it vibrated with energies of flux and reflux. Within an aura of a lambent flame of blue it began to coalesce into a human form, becoming ever clearer, until revealing itself as Isis of Avalon, Queen of Heaven, Spirit of the Moon, whose cosmic love and inspiration radiates eternally. Here was the mistress of the tides, the secret silent tides of death and birth, tides of men's souls and dreams and destiny, tides that rise in our hearts and minds.

The tresses of her hair were long and thick and streamed down softly, flowing and curling about her divine neck. On her head she wore as a crown twelve stars entwined with many garlands of flowers. On her forehead shone white and glowing, a round mirror-like full moon disc. On its right and left it was supported by the furrowed coils of rising vipers with ears of corn bristling beside them. Her tunic was of many colours, woven of the finest linen, gleaming multi-coloured, at first glance with snowy whiteness, then yellow like a crocus, rosy-red like a flame. Her cloak was deep black, glistening with sable sheen. It was cast about her, passing under her right arm and brought together on her left shoulder. Part of it hung down like a shield and drooped in many a fold, the whole reaching to the lower edge of her garment with tasselled fringe. Here and there, along its embroidered border, and also on its surface, were scattered sequins of sparkling stars. In their midst the full moon shone forth like a flame of fire. All along the border of that gorgeous robe there was an unbroken garland of all kinds of flowers and fruits. In her right hand she carried a bronze sistrum rattle. In her left was held a golden cup, an alchemical Grail, from which rose a snake. Her soft feet, not hurting the little flowers, were shod with sandals woven of the palm of victory. Perfumes of resinous woods and gums wafted through the air. Out of the timeless she had come down into time. Out of the un-named she had come down into human symbols. In the land that had called her, amidst the people whose hearts she alone can fill, she was calling forth the flame of the hearts of all. Thus she abided. A thing of beauty and a joy forever.

Extending her right arm, she shook her sistrum, sounding soft celestial bells. From it, like falling stars floating to earth, a sparkling shower of crystalline moon blessings descended, touching the whole of the sacred landscape, resonating through its multitudinous aethyrs, all touching, all penetrant. The Tor maze began to glow ever more strongly and pulsate. The moonlit sparkling Abbey hummed as the face of Isis of Avalon was also seen in the Mary Chapel. All across the land fell the glory of the stars into the hearts of men. The Chalice Well, its cover open, reflected in its water the holy face as the ground seemed to exhale in a great relaxation. Spreading out and touching the Wearyall Hill thorn, to Bride's Mound and beyond, out in all directions the gratuitous grace extended, until finally, the outlines of the signs of the Glastonbury Zodiac were seen, brightly glowing and energised.

At the top of the column of light that was descending into the maze centre, a blue point of light appeared and grew bigger, beginning to descend the same path as the column. It floated down slowly towards the Tor, as Isis of Avalon beamed her grace upon it. A babe in an egg of blue. The New Aeon, the New Age. Coming to birth as its devotees in Glastonbury send healing and magick out unto the entire world and beyond; yea out unto the entire world and beyond.

I have repeated the Burrow Mump Anubis visualisation on a number of other occasions, primarily during journeys along the Michael ley line. It retains its power every time and continues to give the impression to those present of something that is already at the location being seen rather than simply created by normal imagination.

Note. Isis of Avalon is the name of an Iseum of the Fellowship of Isis focused by Celia Thomas.

BIBLIOGRAPHY

Ashe, Geoffrey, *The Ancient Wisdom,* Macmillan, London, 1977.

Ashe, Geoffrey, *Avalonian Quest,* Methuen, London, 1982.

Bennett, Colin, *Looking for Orthon,* Paraview Press, New York, 2001.

Benham, Patrick, *The Avalonians,* Gothic Image, Glastonbury, 1993.

Brown, Rosemary Alicia, *Katherine Emma Maltwood Artist 1878-1961,* Sono Nis Press, Victoria, BC, Canada, 1981.

Bryant, Nigel, Translator, *The High Book of the Grail,* D. S. Brewer, Cambridge, 1996.

Caine, Mary, *The Glastonbury Zodiac,* Surrey, 1978.

Clarke, David, & Roberts, Andy, *Flying Saucerers - A Social History of UFOlogy,* Alternative Albion, Loughborough, UK, 2007.

Collins, Andrew, *The Knights of Danbury,* Earthquest Books, Essex, 1985.

Collins, Andrew, *The Seventh Sword,* Random Century Ltd., London, 1991.

Collins, Andrew, *The Circle Makers,* ABC Books, Essex, 1992.

Collins, Andrew, *From the Ashes of Angels,* Michael Joseph, London, 1996.

Collins, Andrew, *Gods of Eden,* Headline, London, 1998.

Collins, Andrew, *Twenty-First Century Grail,* Virgin, London, 2004.

http://www.andrewcollins.com/page/articles/Gods, Grails and Morphian Contact.htm

Collins, Andrew, *Beneath the Pyramids,* 4th Dimension Press, ARE, USA, 2009.

Collins, Andrew, *LightQuest,* Eagle Wing Books Inc., Memphis, USA, 2012.

Constable, Trevor, James, *The Cosmic Pulse of Life,* Neville Spearman Ltd., UK, 1977

Coon, Robert, *Elliptical Navigations through the Multitudinous Aethyrs of Avalon,* Excalibur Press, Somerset, 1984.

Coon, Robert, *Voyage to Avalon,* Griffon Gold Publications, Somerset, 1986.

Coon, Robert, *Glastonbury and the Planetary New Jerusalem,* Excalibur Press, Glastonbury, 1990.

Coon, Robert, *The Glastonbury Zodiac,* Avalon, 1993.

Coon, Robert, *The Cairo Working,* Glastonbury, 1997.

Dewey, Steve, & Ries, John, *In Alien Heat,* Anomalist Books, UK, 2005.

Elstob, Lynne and Howes, Anne, *The Glastonbury Festivals,* Gothic Image, Glastonbury, 1987.

Forbes, John Foster, *The Unchronicled Past,* Simkin Marshall Ltd., 1938.

Fortune, Dion, *Avalon of the Heart,* London, 1934.

Gennaro, Gino, *The Phenomena of Avalon, The Story of this Planet as Recounted by the Fairies,* Cronos Press, 1979.

Godwin, Joscelyn, *Atlantis and the Cycles of Time,* Inner Traditions, Vermont, 2011.

Heselton, Philip, *Tony Wedd. New Age Pioneer,* Northern Earth Mysteries, Hull, 1986.

Inglesby, Eric, *UFO's and the Christian,* Regency Press, London, 1978.

Jenkins, Stephen, *The Undiscovered Country,* Neville Spearman, Sudbury, Suffolk, UK, 1976.

Jung, C. G., *Flying Saucers,* Princeton University Press, USA, 1978.

Keel, John, *Operation Trojan Horse,* G. P. Putnams Sons, New York, 1970.

Keel, John, *The Mothman Prophecies,* Dutton, New York, 1975.

Leitch, Yuri, *Gwyn,* Temple Publications, Somerset, 2007.

Leitch, Yuri, Ed., *Signs and Secrets of the Glastonbury Zodiac,* Avalonian Aeon Publications, UK, 2013.

Leslie, Desmond, & Adamski, George, *Flying Saucers Have Landed,* Werner Laurie, London, 1953.

Maltwood, Katherine, E. *A Guide to Glastonbury's Temple of the Stars,* James Clarke & Co., Cambridge, 1934.

Maltwood, Katherine, E., *The Enchantments of Britain,* James Clarke & Co., Cambridge, 1944.

Mann, Nicholas, R., *The Isle of Avalon,* Llewellyn, USA, 1996.

Michell, John, *The Flying Saucer Vision,* Sidgwick & Jackson Ltd., UK, 1967.

Michell, John, *The View Over Atlantis,* Sago Press, Great Britain, 1969.

Michell, John, *City of Revelation,* Abacus, UK, 1972.

Michell, John, *New Light on the Ancient Mystery of Glastonbury,* Gothic Image, Glastonbury, 1990.

Pauwels, Louis, & Bergier, Jacques, *The Morning of the Magicians,* Editions Gallimard, France, 1960.

Reiser, Oliver, *This Holyest Erthe,* Perennial Books, London, 1974.

Roberts, Anthony, *Atlantean Traditions in Ancient Britain,* Rider, UK, 1977.

Roberts, Anthony, *Sowers of Thunder,* Rider, UK, 1978.

Roberts, Anthony, Ed., *Glastonbury. Ancient Avalon, New Jerusalem.* Rider & Co., London, 1978.

Roberts, Anthony, *Geomancy,* Zodiac House Publications, Glastonbury, UK, 1980.

Roberts, Anthony, & Gilbertson, Geoff, *The Dark Gods,* Rider/Hutchinson & Co., UK, 1980.

Shuttlewood, Arthur, *The Warminster Mystery,* Neville Spearman Ltd., UK, 1967.

Spence, Lewis, *The Mysteries of Britain,* Senate, Middlesex, 1994.

Trench, Brinsley le Poer, *The Sky People,* Neville Spearman Ltd., London, 1960.

Trench, Brinsley le Poer, *Men Among Mankind,* Neville Spearman Ltd., London, 1962.

Vallee, Jacques, *Passport to Magonia,* Neville Spearman Ltd., UK, 1970.

Van Buren, Elizabeth, *Lord of the Flame,* Neville Spearman, Sudbury, Suffolk, UK, 1981.

Various, *From Atlantis to Avalon and Beyond,* Zodiac House Publications, Glastonbury, UK, 1990.

Various, *Glastonbury & Britain - A Study in Patterns,* RILKO, London, 1990.

Weston, Paul, *Avalonian Aeon,* Avalonian Aeon Publications, Glastonbury, UK, 2010.

Williamson, Tom, & Bellamy, Liz, *Ley Lines in Question,* World's Work Ltd., Surrey, 1983.

Note. The unpublished Anthony Roberts manuscript *Giants in the Earth* has been a fundamental inspiration to this book.

Thanks also to Philip Heselton for information concerning Tony Wedd.

SEE OVERLEAF FOR
OTHER BOOKS FROM
AVALONIAN AEON PUBLICATIONS

MYSTERIUM ARTORIUS

Arthurian Grail Glastonbury Studies

An Introduction & Evocation

PAUL WESTON

MYSTERIUM ARTORIUS

Arthurian Grail Glastonbury Studies

An Introduction & Evocation

is a historical and cultural esoteric extravaganza introducing and evoking Arthur and the Grail through the magic of the landscape and the sensibilities of artists and mystics from the ancient to the modern world.

FEATURING PLACES PHYSICAL AND FABLED:
Glastonbury, Tintagel, Hyperborea, Shambhala, Wewelsburg, Cadbury Castle, Gothic cathedrals, Hall of Chivalry, Grail mountains, Camelot Castle Hotel, Tor labyrinth, Glastonbury Zodiac, New Jerusalem.

MYTHIC FIGURES:
Fulcanelli, Prester John, Melkin, Morgan La Fey, Melchizedek, the Wandering Jew, the Wild Hunt, the Lord of the World.

THE WONDERS OF THE TWELFTH CENTURY:
Knights Templar, Troubadours, Sufism, Hermetica, Henry II, Eleanor of Aquitaine, Abbot Suger, Henry of Blois, Hildegard of Bingen, Bernard of Clairvaux, Joachim of Fiore.

TWENTIETH CENTURY VISIONARIES:
Dion Fortune, John Cowper Powys, Katharine Maltwood, Frederick Bligh Bond, Geoffrey Ashe, Ralph Vaughan Williams, Rudyard Kipling, Flavia Anderson, PD Ouspensky, Jessie Weston, Hank Harrison, Walter Johannes Stein, Edward Elgar, Arnold Bax, Rene Guenon, Rudolf Steiner, Frederick Thomas Glasscock, John Michell.

AND, OF COURSE:
Geoffrey of Monmouth, Chretien de Troyes, Wolfram von Eschenbach, Perlesvaus, Joseph of Arimathea, Arthur's grave.

CONTAINS NO BLOODLINE CONSIDERATIONS AND NO THEORIES IN FAVOUR OF ANY SPECIFIC GRAIL ARTEFACTS

ISBN: 978-0-9557696-0-3

ALEISTER CROWLEY
AND THE AEON OF HORUS

History · Magick · Psychedelia · UFOlogy

PAUL WESTON

ALEISTER CROWLEY
AND THE AEON OF HORUS
History • Magick • Psychedelia • UFOlogy

Is another historical and cultural
esoteric extravaganza from Paul Weston
An Aeon of Horus primer: from the Nazis to
the atom bomb, LSD, and UFOlogy.

BEYOND THE LEGEND OF INFAMY

Aleister Crowley the occult superstar, yogi, mountaineer, junkie, sexual adventurer, and mystical poet, the supreme prophet of the modern world?

ALSO FEATURING

Jack Parsons, L. Ron Hubbard, Marjorie Cameron, JFC Fuller, Hitler, Jacques Vallée, Charles Manson, Timothy Leary, Guido von List,Meade Layne, Robert Anton Wilson, Phillip K. Dick, Gerald Gardner, Rudolf Hess, H. P. Lovecraft, Rudolf Steiner, George Hunt Williamson,Anton Szandor LaVey, Wilhelm Reich, Gurdjieff, the Beatles, Robert Graves, George Van Tassell, Kenneth Grant, Alex Sanders, William Dudley Pelley, C.G. Jung, Kenneth Anger, Aldous Huxley, John Keel.

DEALING WITH DIVERSE AND EXTRAORDINARY SUBJECTS

Babalon Working, Sirius Mystery, Stele of Revealing, psychedelicsixties, Church of Satan, Process Church of the Final Judgement, rebirth of Witchcraft, Manson murders, Thule, orgone energy, Abraxas, Mothman, Illuminati, Men in Black, Gnostic revival, Nazi Occultism, Montauk, Loch Ness monster, Necronomicon, the psychology, magick, and mysticism of Thelema, the crossing of the abyss, secret cipher, Extra-Terrestrial Gnosis.

ISBN: 978-0-9557696-4-1

AVALONIAN AEON
From Glastonbury Festival to 2012
A Personal Occult Odyssey
PAUL WESTON

AVALONIAN AEON

From Glastonbury Festival to 2012

A Personal Occult Odyssey

is an epic and encyclopaedic exposition of the total Glastonbury experience in the form of an autobiographical tale of magic and mysticism, ecstasy, hilarity, horror, the mystery of destiny, the charisma of landscape.

Against the backdrop of Crowley's Aeon of Horus, the Thatcher years, and Gulf War, feeding on a diet of drugs and books, the author was pulled via the famous festival into the mystery of Glastonbury with its history and mythology of the Tor, Arthur and the Grail, Joseph of Arimathea, abbey, Chalice Well, and alleged terrestrial zodiac.

FEATURES:
a misspent youth, outlandish perplexing paranormal phenomena,psychic abilities and manifestations, visions, and artefact retrievals.

INCLUDES:
Early days and inspirations behind the Stonehenge and Glastonbury festivals. Extensive previously unpublished Andrew Collins material providing a unique overview of psychic questing, including the entire story of the seven swords of Meonia and how Glastonbury proved to be a doorway to the mysteries of what may lie beneath the Giza plateau. Complete survey of work of American visionary Robert Coon relating to Glastonbury, Crowley, global chakra sites, and the Omega Point. Green Stone, Sirius, Tintagel, Stele of Revealing, witchcraft, Tarot, Qabalah, Rebirthing, Fellowship of Isis, Harmonic Convergence, Synchronicity.

ALSO STARRING A FURTHER ILLUSTRIOUS CAST OF CHARACTERS:
Dion Fortune, Geoffrey Ashe, José Arguelles, John Cowper Powys, Gurdjieff, John Michell, Leonard Orr, Anthony Roberts, Oliver Reiser, Katherine Maltwood, Frederick Bligh Bond, Graham Phillips, Mary Caine, Robert Anton Wilson, Shirdi Sai Baba, Hank Harrison.

WARNING: THIS BOOK MAY ALTER YOUR STATE OF CONSCIOUSNESS.

ISBN: 978-0-9557696-2-7